Vince has dedicated his life to serving God and serving others. Order this book for anyone who needs help overcoming their past.

TAMMY KLING
CEO, ONFIRE BOOKS LEADERSHIP COMPANY & *NEW YORK TIMES* BEST-SELLING AUTHOR

Child of the King *by Vincent Nelson is a remarkable book—a beautiful, honest, and stirring story of failure, loss, faith, forgiveness, and redemption that takes the reader from the dark depths of a jail cell to the soaring summit of Mt. Kilimanjaro and beyond. I highly recommend this inspiring book, which will touch your heart and give meaning to your life.*

DOUGLAS PRESTON
#1 BEST-SELLING AUTHOR

Raw and real, offering freedom to be authentically you without fear.

STEVE COCKRAM
COFOUNDER, GIANT WORLDWIDE
AUTHOR AND INTERNATIONAL SPEAKER

Our walk with God isn't what we expect. It often feels more like a climb up a steep slope. Our expectations of life's journey betray us with their promises of easy paths, shortcuts to the top, and safe trails without ledges. Vincent Nelson has made this climb and has discovered firsthand the devastation from chasing false summits. But unlike many people who have stumbled, he has kept climbing with God—and he reminds us that we can do the same. If you've ever had deep regrets in your walk with the Lord, Child of the King *can help you learn to see your failures as a toehold to greater heights for His glory.*

WAYNE STILES
AUTHOR OF *WAITING ON GOD: WHAT TO DO WHEN GOD DOES NOTHING*

Healthy authenticity that resonates and invites us on a journey of self-discovery as we join in the author's incredible journey! A rare treat and a true page-turner!

DR. SHANNAN CRAWFORD
CLINICAL PSYCHOLOGIST & CEO OF DR. CRAWFORD AND ASSOCIATES

This book is real and raw—an authentic look at one man's journey to discover his own self-worth!

SCOTT GRAHAM
SENIOR PASTOR, BETHEL LIFE CHURCH

I'm incredibly grateful God used the last days of my brother's life on Mt. Kilimanjaro to give Vince the courage to share his story in a transparent way. It is my prayer that Vince's story will impact the lives of others, leading many to the freedom to live the incredible destiny that's waiting to be lived.

KAREN BYERLY KESSINGER
SISTER OF ALAN BYERLY, FELLOW MT. KILIMANJARO CLIMBER

This is a book a father will pass on to his children, creating waves of impact among generations; profoundly guiding every reader through layers of bondage into freedom's open arms.

LINDSAY WEIR
CEO OF THE BETTER BABE PROJECT

With my travels around the world I've seen that every human begin has two fundamental needs...to be loved and find meaning in life. My friend Vince Nelson has discovered the path to experiencing both of these through his own journey of brokenness and healing while climbing Mt. Kilimanjaro. If you're on a journey to discover love, honor, purpose and significance for your life, then I encourage you to read Child of the King.

BRIAN TIBBS
CEO EXTREME NAZARENE MINISTRIES

Child
—of—
The King

*Discover the Honor, Purpose,
and Destiny within You*

Vincent Nelson

Carpenter's Son Publishing

Child of the King: Discover the Honor, Purpose, and Destiny within You

©2017 Vincent Nelson

Published by Carpenter's Son Publishing, Franklin, Tennessee

Published in association with Larry Carpenter of Christian Book Services, LLC
www.christianbookservices.com

Cover and interior design by Suzanne Lawing

Edited by Tammy Kling

Printed in the United States of America

978-1-942587-96-5

Hell found me and permeated my soul.
But heaven embraced me and told hell no!

—Vincent Nelson

CONTENTS

ACKNOWLEDGMENTS

To the King:
I reflect back on the journey of my life, and my heart is filled with gratitude. I'm grateful because through all my failure, my Creator and King loved me through it all, never leaving me, gently leading me, always loving me, finally helping me to rest and be the dearly loved son that I am to him.

To my wife:
Thank you for loving me and giving me the courage to live in truth, love, and transparency and to share my story. Without you, I would never have written and shared the story on these pages. I'm grateful for every day we walk together on the road less traveled, the path of truth and love...our intimacy journey.

To my boys:
Simon, thank you for teaching me to how see through others' eyes. You are a man full of courage and love. Nick, you've learned the secret to what real power in life is, listening and receiving from the King. Live every day with that kind of heart. I'm proud of you both.

To Tammy:
Thank you for speaking life into me so I can share it with others.

To my Celebrate Recovery brothers:
Through you I learned what real intimacy looks like…living
in stark truth, no hiding, bold courage spoken and lived out.
In the revealing of our darkest secrets, the light of love and
honor replaced fear and shame. Freedom was found…a place
of being fully known, knowing another completely, and still
being loved and embraced.

To Dan:
Thank you for loving me enough to speak truth and confront
the darkness of my heart and the chains that caused me to
live life as a prisoner for decades. The truth you spoke freed
me to begin the deeper truth journey of the soul.

To Billy:
Thank you for wiping the tears from my eyes and the snot
from my nose, and for embracing me as a dearly loved son
when I was broken. You showed me what real love is.

To Mike and Steve:
Thank you for modeling and teaching a
different way of being a Christian. Thank you for
discipling me in a way that led to finding rest and
living as a dearly loved son of the King.

To my dad and mom:
Thank you, Dad, for showing me what love is, and Mom, for
showing me what wisdom is. Thank you for walking through
some of the most difficult days of my life.

FOREWORD

In *Child of the King* Vince Nelson takes us on a journey of discovery, one we all need to engage with—a journey into understanding our God-given identity.

All of us need to understand the basis of our identity as children of God. Without the confidence that such an understanding brings, we may wrestle with issues of personal security and significance. We may even falter in our attempts to make good decisions, even about ordinary things. Without confidence, life can so easily slide into a series of unbearable struggles.

So if confidence is so important, where does it come from? It comes from clarity about our identity. Such clarity will always give birth to confidence, and this kind of confidence will always lead to courage. And surely we all need courage to live our lives with purpose.

From Alighieri Dante (*The Divine Comedy*) to John Bunyan (*Pilgrim's Progress*) and from C. S. Lewis (*The Chronicles of Narnia*) to William P. Young (*The Shack*), Christian writers have been using imagery and allegory to teach us the deepest lessons of life. Vince is no different. His rich narrative style draws us from the lowest valley of human failure to the highest peak of Christian revelation—a peak from which the beautiful vista of our identity in Christ breaks upon us.

I'm sure *Child of the King* will be a gift to all who follow Vince from the valley of "the shadow" to the "mountaintop" of God's richest blessing.

MICHAEL BREEN
Founder of 3DM and author of
Building a Discipling Culture

PREFACE

My heart is filled with great expectation as a new journey begins for me. It's a journey of living in complete love and truth, in complete vulnerability, with the hope that as I share this book with you and many others, you will experience for yourself a different kind of life than you've perhaps been living.

My hope is that you will live a life filled with excitement and purpose. It's a life filled with power as you live out the magnificent destiny you were designed with—a destiny this world needs and only you can bring.

If you've felt like a failure, you can finally forgive yourself and live a full life. If you've struggled to make things happen, you'll finally be able to rest. As you slow down and enjoy life, you'll see you were more productive than you were before.

It's the kind of life where the rejected find acceptance and embrace—where you finally believe you are loved and you're lovable, you are valuable and you make a difference.

The mountain is in your head.

—Bethany Williams

Chapter 1

LIFE IN CAPTIVITY

The concrete floor was cold and damp, the unshakeable kind of cold that chills your bones until they hurt. Without a blanket, I lay there and stared at the ceiling. There were no windows or warmth from the sunlight, just an intimidating solid steel door demanding my submission. As I pondered my surroundings, I felt as lifeless as the cold jail cell. I was a prisoner before I ever came to this cell. A prisoner of my own stupidity, destroying every shred of dignity and honor I had left.

Hour after hour went by with nothing but deafening silence, and an occasional voice echoing obscenities down the hallway. I couldn't see the faces of others, but I could hear one inmate, a lost soul who expressed his extreme discontentment.

As I lay there, I realized my prison wasn't limited to those cement walls. My jail cell extended beyond this space into my life, my marriage, and my job. I had been a prisoner for decades.

Tears began to pour out, bringing a sense of enormous loss and painful regrets. I reflected on all the gifts I knew I had but were marred by the regret of what I'd done. I'd been an influential pastor of several large churches for seventeen years. I thought of my two amazing boys, and how I'd once had a loving wife.

My resume and hard work rolled before my eyes like a movie reel in my mind. I had led a large staff and traveled the world, building businesses and ministries to launch tens of thousands of churches. Throughout everything I had built a good name and reputation. Even so, I lost all of it through my own terrible disdain for myself.

Still deep in contemplation, I thought about the woman I tried to impress the night before by drinking way too much and getting pulled over. I knew I wouldn't be able to escape a DWI charge now.

Come Monday morning, I didn't know if I'd still have my investment advisor job. The crazy thing was, I didn't drink. I know, all alcoholics say this, but I actually didn't. However, I was addicted to the thought of meeting my needs on my own terms in order to feel more significant. *Impress good-looking women. That's what I need.* Or so I thought. Now all I wanted to do was kick myself in the head.

Thousands of thoughts wreaked havoc in my mind, competing for space with regret. A thought, a memory, a regret. It was a circular and silent conversation.

I knew I had a great family. I knew I had incredible opportunities in the church, being able to make a difference all around the world. So why? Why did I have that affair? Why didn't I ever seek counseling to prevent the affair? Even when the church board found out, they were incredibly gracious to my family and me and asked me to stay and work through it. I knew I couldn't heal if I stayed. I was so broken. I was so messed up. I wanted to work through my issues for my family, so I resigned.

My wife had committed to work through the affair and stay married. So why after that, even after receiving some of the best counseling in the world, did I still strive to communicate with the woman I had the affair with? I was seeking attention from someone I never intended to build a life with, and I knew something was terribly broken inside of me to cause me to hurt others and self-destruct. Once my wife found out I contacted the woman again, divorce was certain. I remember crying for hours knowing the impending heartache my boys were about to experience, the same broken heart I had experienced when I became a child of divorce. It was the same thing I swore they would never have to live through.

Communication with those who were closest to me faded and inevitably ceased. I felt isolated and alone. I realized I had hurt many who trusted in me. I lied to them and wasn't honest about the affair when asked, so unfortunately they had to find out from others. I was hiding the truth of what was really going on inside my heart because I knew how bad I was. Truthfully, I felt so much shame; I couldn't fathom revealing that to anyone.

I was the one who pushed away those who loved me. An even deeper layer of truth: I hadn't ever let anyone all the way into my life because I never thought I was worthy of being loved.

I felt like a failure having to move from Indiana back to Texas, where my family was. Any sense of a good name I had was flushed away like a piece of toilet paper. I just lost my job. For decades I poured my life into ministry. I felt like a hero helping thousands of people all over the world. I found great meaning and significance through my work. It became an addictive drug I sought after more and more.

So I would do bigger and bigger endeavors at the church. I remember at one point being responsible for a staff of fifty people, running a financial campaign to raise three million dollars, giving sermons weekly, and working on a project in Argentina to build a hotel and convention center to fund the start-up of fifty thousand churches in the Amazon region of South America. How crazy was that? That was way too much for anyone to take on, and I knew it.

The stress was incredible. I would often remind God of everything I was doing for him, so couldn't he make my life easier? I know, me telling God what to do was crazy, but I'm just being honest. I was a pastor and knew better, but I was learning that knowledge wasn't enough to change me.

For the first time in my life, I realized all the theological training, the vast amount of knowledge of God, of right and wrong and how to live a moral life, hadn't created a lasting heart change within me.

Greater understanding of life, even of God, hadn't given me what I needed to love myself and love others the right way. The only thing adding more knowledge did was create a greater awareness of my selfishness, and my inability to realize the nobility I had heard God say was within me.

When I was a child, my friends and I would often play a game at the beach, seeing who could hold the beach ball under the waves the longest. The farther you push it down, the harder it is to keep it down as tremendous pressure builds. Inevitably the pressure of the ocean and

> LIKE TRYING TO HOLD A BEACH BALL UNDER THE OCEAN WAVES, SOUL ISSUES NOT DEALT WITH EVENTUALLY POP UP TO BE SEEN BY ALL.
>
> —VINCENT NELSON

the hidden undercurrent on the ball would cause it to pop up, often in unpredictable ways, smacking us painfully in the face. The same was true of the issues I wanted to hide. The more I tried to hide them, the sooner and harder they would pop up in selfish actions, like an affair. I couldn't find a clear path to freedom and peace. Ministry didn't do it. Working out didn't do it. The affair didn't do it.

All the childhood pain of my past would slip out of my controlled suppression and pop up at the worst times and in the worst ways. Vivid emotional images would resurface of being sexually abused by a female babysitter, stealing my sense of safety and innocence as a child. And lingering images of the little girl I became sexually active with when I was only seven years old, who showed me things most people don't know how to do even as adults, would carousel in my thoughts.

Looking back, I now know she must have been a victim of sexual abuse herself. All of these things increased my sexual desire while at the same time making me feel immeasurable shame. I felt that if people knew the real me, they would see the disgusting, dirty little boy I believed I was. All of this happened under my dad's watch, who divorced my mom when I was five. I began wondering who was there to protect me.

During those years in Houston, my dad had taken full custody of me. He was working most of the time, which made it extremely hectic for me growing up. My dad was one of the most successful photographers in Houston, which meant I was left alone a lot on the weekends and evenings, letting myself in and out, cooking for myself, and finding ways to creatively pass the time.

Every other weekend and in the summers, I'd spend time with my mom. That proved to be even more chaotic at times. When my mom and dad split up, she chose a female partner, which you can imagine created a lot of confusion as a young boy growing up. While there were good memories, there were also the images of rage, as she and her lover would often threaten each other with knives.

Where there should have been an atmosphere of love and nurture as a child, there were deep-seated fears of mortal harm that I always felt when she'd point her finger at me. In my young mind, her finger morphed into the same knife that she would use to threaten her lover. Reflecting back, I know my mother loved me, and she even showed it in many ways. Still, the embedded fears from those early childhood experiences would stay with me for years to come. All of those gaping untreated soul wounds only grew worse without treatment.

One of my greatest failures was not seeking help from others. I was trying, in my own might, to protect myself. This method led to an addiction of epic proportion in trying to meet my needs independently. In a lot of ways, as I grew into a man, I was still a child. I felt dirty and broken, without honor, without purpose, trying to hide in a corner where the world couldn't see, touch, or hurt the real me.

As I grew into a man, I focused my life's purpose on becoming honorable and doing good things in an attempt to reveal meaning in my life. I wanted my life to be worth something, and I was going to do whatever it took to make that happen. So the discovery of God was a great way to feed my addiction for just that. I sought his love. I needed it, but the deeper issue was that I never allowed God's love to pursue me.

In the depths of my soul, hidden where no one could see, was the broken little boy who never healed, and grew up with a deeply rooted need to prove to God and others that he was worth something. I had to prove that to myself. So I was determined to make a name for myself, with God and with others.

I had become a well-respected pastor who knew he should live a moral life. I wasn't supposed to drink. I wasn't supposed to be a workaholic. So I ended up exchanging one addiction for another, becoming a workout fanatic to medicate my sense of self-worth. It even worked for a while: exercising three hours a day, I became super strong. I was running marathons, and in my early forties I looked the best I had ever looked in my life. But running wasn't just about looking good; it was also about running from the pain I hadn't confronted.

Several years earlier, my son, Simon, was diagnosed with autism. I remember the first time my wife and I were told: "Your son has autism."

A doctor said, "He'll always have autism and will never change." I was devastated. I didn't fully understand what it meant for his life, but I knew it was horrific. I'd seen the movie *Rain Man*. Would this now become Simon? At once, every dream I had for my beautiful three-year-old boy was shattered. He'd never get married, never go to college, and never do normal things like play baseball with other kids.

The pain was overwhelming; I couldn't face it. Having hundreds of people come up to me at church saying how sorry they were for us made me all the more aware I was living in a fish bowl, and I felt terribly vulnerable and exposed; I had to hide. So I buried the emotion ball deeper and tried my best to be a father, husband, pastor, and whatever else was needed. While my intentions were to help my family, locking up my emotions further eroded intimacy in my marriage.

Hiding, running, feeding addictions that might be acceptable to most as "lesser sins" all led down the self-centered path to the affair, the one that was the beginning of the end. Even in the affair, I was once again trying to manipulate the situation to make me feel better about myself.

So I did the very thing I hated to keep the affair going—I became a liar and cheater. I was even further away from what I wanted to be: a man of honor and worth. What I believed about myself on the inside was beginning to be visible on the outside. No matter what I did, it was never enough to prove I was valuable. There were always stains on my life that never went away.

I began to hate ministry and get discouraged, believing I would never experience peace, no matter how much I could do for people and God. I was growing discontent at home. I wanted a way out. I hated myself. I was selfish and was growing tired of living an illusionary life that promised peace and purpose but instead was an inescapable prison whose walls only became thicker through a constant demand of greater effort to prove I was worth something, that I was worthy of being loved.

Unable to break free from decades of learning how to meet my needs my way, I tried to reconcile my marriage. Out of a controlling sense of duty and obligation, I sought restoration. Only this time in life, while I understood the word *love*, I was incapable of expressing what I was never able to receive. While I knew the words of love, my words were lifeless. It was now over, and the divorce was inevitable.

Broken, cold, and weeping as I lay on the cement floor of my jail cell, I no longer wanted to protect myself. There was nothing left to protect. The broken little boy that was hidden away from the world was now exposed. Everyone could now see the dark thoughts of my heart. My boys saw their father had failed them.

I was now known as the adulterer, the liar, the selfish father, the failure in ministry. It was all on display. I thought of a quote by Carrie Fisher: "You're only as sick as your secrets." Well, no more hiding. All I had worked for my entire life, to find value and worth, was destroyed. But in that moment, the greatest gift I could have ever received happened. The door of my jail cell opened.

"Vince, Vince wake up. You've been crying in your sleep."

My eyes began to open. I looked up at the orange tent

ceiling. It was still night and freezing.

Bethany poked her head into my tent. "Vince, are you okay?"

"Yes, I believe I am." I wiped away the tears I had cried in my sleep. "The door to my life is now wide open," I said with a smile. "Let's go tackle the summit."

The harder the climb, the more it's going to challenge you, push you and stretch you. Your reward lies on the other side.

—BETHANY WILLIAMS AND VINCENT NELSON

Chapter 2

THE DOOR IS OPEN

It was pitch black. All I could see were about twenty head lamps slowly treading up the side of a pitch-black slope. To keep some semblance of reality, I had to envision what the side of Mount Kilimanjaro looked like in daylight.

All my senses were hypersensitive trying to compensate for the lack of light. I could hear Bethany breathing, and the occasional rock would get knocked over the side of the mountain by some hiking boots.

It was insanely cold too. It took less than an hour for my water bladder to freeze, cutting off our access to water, and we still had another five hours to go before we reached the summit of Africa's lonely mountain—15,000 to 19,300 feet. This was no afternoon hike.

"So what were you crying about last night?" Bethany asked with a weak voice, as the high altitude stole every ounce of oxygen from her words.

"I was dreaming about my past and everything that led up to that jail cell moment," I said. Whew, that was a painful memory, and I relived it in that dream. It felt so real.

"About the affair?" Bethany asked.

"Well yeah, but not just the affair. The DWI, the affair, my stupid decisions in life that lead up to it, and hurting others."

"That's intense," she said. "I'm sorry you had to experience that pain. Why were you smiling then when you said the door to your life is wide open now?"

"Oh that, yeah." I chuckled. "I realized I had been living life in a prison of fear. It was fear of being hurt by others and never allowing anyone to really know me, which caused me to miss out on deep, meaningful relationships for decades, with my ex-wife, with close friends, and others. But I realized at the end of my dream, like the jail cell I was in, the cell door to my life finally opened. I was free. I didn't have to live in fear anymore. There was nothing to hide. After I had got out of jail for the DWI, my freedom walk began at a counseling place called Crazy 8."

Bethany chuckled.

I knew the words crazy and counseling weren't great combinations. Kinda funny actually.

"I know, I know," I said. "Why they named the place Crazy 8 I don't know. However, it was a game changer in my life. It had been three long weeks since I was held captive in that jail cell and my heart was now in a different place, a barren place. I no longer was in hiding, but boy, was I raw. My emotions were like fragile china plates precariously balanced on toothpicks. Anything set me off to feel like a failure and made me want to give up on life."

I asked Bethany, "Have you ever experienced a moment where you cannot grasp hope, or where the future seems uncertain?"

"You mean like I feel at this moment?" she said with a voice full of alarm. "Vince, I need your help!"

Bethany's head lamp was dead. And it was so dark that without her head lamp, it would only take a few steps before she'd fall off the side of the mountain, a few thousand feet down.

Feeling her panic, I immediately repositioned my head lamp to cover both her feet and mine. "Don't worry," I said, walking very close to her. "I'll take care of us both."

I hadn't thought about it until now, but this truly was a life-and-death situation. The higher we got, the dizzier we got from the high elevation. Several times we both caught each other as we stumbled over rocks.

She needed me at this moment. I needed her too. Just like I need others in my life. The fear in her voice subsided as I walked closer to her. I thought back to that moment in the counseling room.

"You know, I think that period in my life was the darkest point in my life," I said to Bethany, "about as dark as it is right now. But all that was about to change."

"Tell me about that day that changed everything," Bethany said. "I need you to distract me, because if I think about how cold it is, how tired my legs are, and how the throbbing, sharp pain in my back jars with every step, I might not make it up this mountain."

"I walked into my first counseling session. There were two counselors there, Lisa and Billy. I guess they thought I needed double the standard help."

Bethany laughed. "Knowing you, I bet you did."

"Yeah, yeah," I said, acknowledging the truth of her comment while shrugging it off. "So Lisa took the role as lead counselor and chit-chatted for a few minutes. But it didn't take long before the floodgates opened. She told me, 'Vince, I get the image of a huge pitcher above your head that God wants to pour into your soul. He wants to pour all of his love and self into you.' Then she asked a simple question: 'Are you ready?'"

Even though I had been a pastor, the thought of charismatic hokey-pokey (people saying, "God wants to do something supernatural") always scared me to death. I've seen people controlling other people by saying, "Thus says the Lord," manipulating them for various reasons. The deeper issue though was that if God was really doing something supernatural, it meant I was about to lose all control, and God would take over. Well, if I allowed God to take over, I wouldn't be in control. My past has shown me if you trust people, you're going to get hurt.

It was different now, though. The jail cell door to my life was open. There was nothing left to hide, and I had nothing left to protect. So I told Lisa, "Sure. I'm ready. I've lost everything anyway. I had nothing of value to give God, so he can do anything he wants."

"So how did that make you feel?" Bethany asked. "Didn't you feel very vulnerable?"

"Yes, I did, in a huge way." But that vulnerability became the open door where I could finally receive the help I had never allowed anyone to give. In that moment, I felt a flood of love pour into my soul, unlike anything I'd ever experienced. I felt embraced by Eternity.

The impenetrable thick prison wall I had built around my heart, built for my protection, had been destroyed in my jail cell with the realization I had nothing left to hide and nothing left to give. For the first time in my life, after "doing" for God for more than three decades, I was finally able to just receive.

Decades of pent-up tears wouldn't stop.

For more than fifteen minutes I basked in God's love. Billy, who would later become an incredible mentor and friend, did something I'll never forget. I had snot running down my face, and he took a box of Kleenex and began wiping it and the tears away.

That simple act helped me experienced these next words. They were words spoken from God's spirit into my soul: "This is my Son, whom I love; with him I am well pleased" (Matthew 3:17 NIV).

Just as I said those words, Bethany said, "Vince, turn around. You've gotta see this."

I slowly turned around, trying to grab the side of the mountain and stabilize myself as every muscle in my body shook with fatigue from having climbed for seven hours.

My jaw dropped. I was breathless. It was truly one of the most profound moments I had ever witnessed. Over the horizon, the curvature of the earth was bending where the red hue of the rising sun split the blackness of the round earth from the dark blue fabric of space dotted with a few stars and a crescent moon.

We had finally reached the summit.

I breathed this moment in. From where I stood at 18,638 feet—the top of the world—on earth's tallest freestanding mountain, I could see everything, not just the plains of Africa below me and the horizon in front of me. I could also see with crystal clarity my past and my present.

Breathing the cleanest air my lungs had ever tasted, I wondered, *Is this what freedom feels like?* I wasn't sure what that really meant, but what I knew was, seven hours into one of the hardest, most strenuous hikes of my entire life, I felt the closest to my Creator than I ever had in my life.

Run towards your fears in order to avoid them.
Facing fears erases them from your story.

—BETHANY WILLIAMS AND VINCENT NELSON

Chapter 3

COMING HOME

It had taken six grueling days to get to this point. We'd gone 30 miles, from 6,000 feet to 18,638 feet, and we'd finally made it to the first summit landing point. As I climbed, I reflected on the last few years of my life. I had come a long way since that jail cell, overcoming an overwhelming lifetime of failure and adversity.

The sun came up quickly, and I could see for hundreds of miles out over the golden African plains below. It was a beautiful cloudless day with crisp air that froze into small condensed, cloud-like wisps before my mouth.

We continued our trek to the second summit point, about 45 minutes ahead, to reach 19,000 feet. We were walking on the top of the mountain. The elevation made every step feel like our legs were twice their normal weight. It was slow going, and hard for us to breathe.

As we trotted our way slowly ahead, I noticed a dormant

volcanic crater off to the right that had been there for thousands of years. We climbed to another spot, and from that point, I could see the peaks of glaciers that had existed for so many years. I couldn't help but stand in awe of the majesty of it all.

How many tens of thousands of people had summited this mountain? Was it a spiritual quest for them too? A rediscovery of their true identity and life purpose?

It's no accident that mountains bring great wisdom and truth and peace and deep revelation about the things of life when you climb. As I scaled that great mountain, I felt the years of disappointment and shame fall away. It was more than the endorphins and the physical aspect of the journey. It was spiritual at the deepest level, and I felt like I was encountering God everywhere along the journey. It felt like it was God's plan for me to scale that mountain.

With every step of the climb, I reflected back on my life since the divorce over three years before. I had begun the journey of believing I was loveable, although I still had a long way to go. I was starting to let go of the shame of the lives I had hurt through my selfishness. Like the sunrise on Kilimanjaro that split the sky from the earth, my Creator's love had split my fear from my heart with the precision of a surgeon's scalpel; I was beginning to receive goodness into my life, for the first time in decades. With courage and a heart finally receiving love, I was moving forward in my life.

I had experienced love through a friend named Billy, a counselor I met during this time of my life, who helped me see the infinite value God saw in me. Billy loved me for who I was, not for what I could or would ever do. He loved me in the darkest place of my life. Bluntly, he loved me when I was at my ugliest, and that became freedom's embrace to my soul. With Billy at my side and a few amazing men from a group called Celebrate Recovery that helped addicts of all kinds find

> BE WILLING TO WALK THROUGH THE VALLEYS WITH OTHERS SO THAT TOGETHER YOU CAN REACH THE SUMMITS.
>
> —BETHANY WILLIAMS AND VINCENT NELSON

healing, I began the incredible journey of learning how to stop trying to meet my needs my way and just allow God to provide. It was with a group of men that many in the world would call losers—former drug addicts, porn addicts, and disposable people—but I called heroes and friends. It was a place where I began the journey of complete vulnerability. A place of being entirely truthful with who I was, failures and all, and finding love and courage amongst a band of brothers.

A profound theme was emerging: life isn't life without others by your side. It had taken a team of forty Sherpas to get ten members of my hiking team up the mountain. It took people helping me at every obstacle to push harder, climb over the boulders in my way, and not give up when I wanted to quit.

"Are we there yet?" Bethany asked, her voice weak with little oxygen to get the words out.

"Look," I said. "There's the second summit point." We had arrived at Stella's Point, which sits 19,012 feet atop Mt Kilimanjaro.

It was beautiful. We were overlooking the volcanic crater below with the glaciers to our right and the clearest blue sky I had ever seen surrounding us.

"Let's shoot the show here," Bethany said. She hosted a television talk show for people in business, and I had the privilege of helping produce and shoot the show. As I was setting up the gear, I realized again, *God, I am so amazingly loved by you, though I still don't know why.*

I had been introduced to Bethany through a mutual friend by the name of Tammy Kling. Tammy is a coach I had met on

Facebook. It was a "God encounter" for sure because I hadn't known her, but felt prompted to reach out to her for coaching when I saw her on social media. It was a big step at the time because I really didn't have the money to pay for a coach, but felt like I was supposed to do it. I took a step in faith and I made that commitment, much like every step up the side of Kilimanjaro was in the dark of night. I sensed there were great things ahead with Tammy, though I wasn't sure what they would be. My goal that day was to simply talk to her about my life and my plan moving forward. As we sat by her outdoor fireplace, she looked into my eyes and listened to what I had to say.

I did not tell her the entire story of my life, but I touched on a few things and how I felt God was leading me. "I'm co-leading a group in the singles ministry at Gateway Church," I said.

Tammy asked me about that, and as she talked, she paused. "Don't date," she said suddenly.

Later she would tell me that God had spoken to her right at that moment with those words and she did not know why.

Even though I wasn't in any rush to date, I'm sure God knew that leading a singles ministry as a single guy would be a massive challenge. Looking back, I can see how God set everything up in advance. How he protected my heart and my mind and prepared me for what was about to occur on the road ahead.

Since I was in no rush to date and thought she probably had some wisdom that I didn't, I heeded her request. After all, I was paying for it! And I was learning, learning to listen to others, especially God, even when it didn't make sense.

Weeks later Tammy called me and told me I needed to meet Bethany Williams, a woman she had met when they were delivering their TEDx talks. What Tammy didn't explain at the time was that God told her to introduce the two of us. Obviously, God had me there for a reason. Again, however, I heeded her advice and reached out to Bethany. We met for the first time in Tammy's living room, the very same place that Tammy had connected another powerful world-changing couple, Nick Vujicic and his wife, Kanae.

Since that introduction, Bethany and I have had an amazing two year journey of sharing failures, fears, struggles, and dreams. As we shared everything with each other, our newfound vulnerability became the glue that would make us best friends. I was no longer alone and learning how to let people in.

I looked up and saw Bethany, and I felt profound gratitude. What are the odds that I would find the love of my life and she would want to climb mountains with me? Listening to others, to God, receiving love...I was beginning to see this was what made life worth living.

"Are you ready?" I asked Bethany.

"Okay, we're rolling in three, two, one and go." Bethany did a great first take, but I had other plans.

"Can you do that one more time, Bethany? I think I had a problem with the camera." I told her to shoot it one more time to get it right.

She was agitated that I would ask her to do it again when she was absolutely exhausted from the climb.

As she was doing her second take, I walked up to her and interrupted her. Getting down on one knee, I proposed to Bethany Williams at the second of three summit points, and my heart was soaring. I never imagined I would be there in that moment.

Time stood still. Even as the proposal rolled off my tongue, a thousand emotions washed over my soul. Feelings of elation, gratitude, even unworthiness hit me in wave after wave. How could I possibly kneel there, before such a beautiful woman, with even a chance of spending my life with her after all the bad I had done? Yet, there I was, and it was happening, almost like I was watching a fairy tale.

"Will you marry me?" I asked.

After what seemed like a long deafening silence, she began to cry. I was a little concerned and repeated myself just to make sure she had really heard me.

"Yes!" she finally said. As I placed the ring on her finger, we both cried. I thanked God for all he had done for me, though I felt like I deserved none of it.

We ascended the mountain as two and descended as one, engaged and with a certainty that we'd never part. It was a great sense of love, peace, and joy.

That joy would be short lived, though.

Shortly after our decent down the mountain began, we learned that our strongest and most inspiring member of our team, Alan Byerly, had died on the summit.

We were in shock. We knew this was no easy hike, but death? Really?

Alan was a highly conditioned athlete and marathon runner. He was a serious yet jovial man and probably the most equipped for the journey. I thought that if anyone would make it, he would.

A few hours later, several others had to be evacuated off the mountain for high altitude sickness. One of our team member's lungs had filled up with fluid, making it impossible to breathe. This condition is called HAPE (high altitude pulmonary edema) we would later learn.

We had to get off the mountain fast, seeing it was more dangerous than any of us had realized. The life-threatening effects of being that high in altitude for that long was taking a very frightening toll on many of our members.

Bethany and I continued the downward trek off the mountain. Kilimanjaro reminded me that life is not a game and never to be taken lightly. I began thinking about Alan's life. He was a man that learned how to receive and give love. His journey had been full with family, friends, and doing the things that he loved, such as running marathons and making a positive difference in the world. Even in the short time we knew him on our trip, Alan had touched all of our lives in a positive way, motivating us to reach the summit. I could never have done it without him pushing us on, and after I had learned of his passing, I was more convicted than ever to finish in his honor.

I wanted my life to be no less impactful. Only this time, I realized the journey had to begin a different way. It wasn't about all the things I could ever do for the sake of greatness. It wasn't even about all the lives I could touch with compassion. The journey this time had to begin with being who I was created to be. Only, who was I and what if I messed up again and lost Bethany? How could I ever trust myself again?

This time the journey would be about receiving the value my Creator says I have, and then valuing myself and valuing others. Yet there was a gnawing feeling inside of me that I had no clue how to do that. Seventeen years of ministry and I still was missing something. Clearly all the religious training I had wasn't enough to answer the deepest questions about my identity and why I chose such a destructive path. For too long my life had been about valuing myself the way others viewed me.

Early in life, I couldn't see beyond what the world's expectations of a man's life were. Many of us are raised by parents where you are rewarded for certain actions. So we live life thinking that we have to perform a certain way to receive love. Then we live that same way as adults. *Perform, and you'll be rewarded.* We believe, *If I perform and do well enough, then I'll be acceptable...then I'll be loved.* For me, that created a chameleon persona that shifted like sand, becoming what people valued, not who I really was.

A greater problem was that even when I tried to ignore

what others said and tried to focus on whatever sort of value I had within, my self-spoken negative words would sabotage my life. Before I applied to a job, I would think about my limitations and talk myself out of interviewing.

Whenever there would be a girl I would want to date as a teenager, I'd think about all the reasons she wouldn't like me, and I'd talk myself out of calling her. After the affair and divorce, up until that point, I had lived life in self-defeat, and I was ready for a change.

"Are you okay, Vince?" Bethany yelled, from about five yards ahead.

"Yes, baby, just thinking about Alan, how I want to live the rest of my life, and wondering how can I ever get there."

"Okay. Well, I'm going to try to catch up to the guide, so don't fall far behind," Bethany said. With that, she took off ahead.

I looked behind me, and no one was there. At that moment I was alone, but it was okay. It just gave me more time to think as I walked down the mountain.

Every step I took down the mountain into the jungle and into the open plains of Africa took me on a journey back to another time—a time of kings, knights, noblemen, honor, and valor. My mind raced to *Gladiator*, one of my favorite movies, where Russell Crow as General Maximus boldly spoke these words before battle: "What we do in life echoes in eternity."

YES! My heart leaped with excitement.

I wanted a significant life that meant something; only this time it would take a different road to get there. I knew the old path of doing more to be significant wouldn't work; it had destroyed me. Yes, as I thought of the words of Maximus, I knew there had to be more to life that I was missing.

I thought of the courage General Maximus poured into his army, his men, and his friends. "Strength and honor!" he declared to them before the battle.

Ah yes, the warrior call! It wasn't that Maximus was telling his men to suck it up and manufacture strength and honor for the fight ahead. Instead, he was pointing out what his men already had within. Maximus was calling them to see the value they already possessed. He was calling them to see it for themselves and embrace it. This was the secret place in a warrior's heart that Maximus knew would free his men to experience victory. I wondered if this would make a difference in my life.

As I was beginning to leave the jungle of Kilimanjaro behind, I heard the voice of a familiar friend speak to me. This is the same friend who had been with me since the beginning, always speaking truth to me, encouraging me to make wise decisions and learn. Now, my friend wasn't someone who could be seen. And no, I wasn't losing my mind. Call it "God," "the Spirit," my conscience, or whatever you want to. All I knew at the time was that it sounded like a quiet whisper within my soul, which often sounded like my own voice.

My Friend began to ask a few questions. "Vince, doesn't God, being the Creator of all things, have infinite worth? Meaning if he created all things, then he would have the greatest value?"

Well, of course, I thought. *God is God, and there is no one greater, so yes, he has the greatest value of all.*

Then my Friend asked, "Vince, if you have been made in God's image, then don't you possess God's worth and value? And if you do possess his worth, why haven't you lived like it? Why haven't you valued yourself and not short-changed yourself, settling for illusions of love that you try to control, that aren't love at all? You're worth so much more, aren't you?"

My mind began swirling with too many thoughts to recount. My feet were continuing the hike, but my heart gasped for answers. I know God has infinite worth. I know God loves me. He values me enough to make me in his image, so why have I never been able to receive his love and see myself the way he sees me?

My Friend continued, "Vincent, you are dearly loved. Not once have you ever not been loved by God. You've only been unloved by yourself. I've asked you a lot of questions to reflect on, but now I ask you an even greater question. Now that you are beginning to receive the value God says you have, what will your life look like as you live as a dearly loved son of the King of the Universe? What destiny is there that you can't accomplish as a child of the King?"

I was gasping for air. And this time it wasn't the high altitude that was causing breathlessness; it was the overwhelming sense that there was so much more to life than I had ever seen or felt.

What does it mean to be a son of the King, to be made in his image? My mind continued to reflect on my Friend's words. As I hiked, the heavy armor I had built for self-protection as a child began to come off, and I could almost feel my soul grow lighter. It was as if a breastplate of self-righteousness and self-justification, one I wore to validate my value and worth to others and myself, dropped off along the hiking trail. It was rusted on the inside, especially the part of the breastplate close to my heart. In its place a tender open heart was revealed.

It was an incredibly vulnerable feeling, but I was becoming much lighter and could feel my stride pick up. I could feel freedom, and it felt good!

I no longer had the need to hide from what was true about myself. Yes, I had an affair, I was a liar and a manipulator, and it was horrific. It caused terrible damage to many.

My heart was broken over it, but my failure didn't unmake me a son of the King. I was still loved. And a thought that was even harder to receive but was true was this: I still carried my King's value, his honor, because I carried his DNA within me. I was made in his image. It wasn't my honor. My honor was my self-righteousness, which was ugly, dark, and hurtful to others.

This time I was going to try to take the right path and leave self-righteousness behind.

All self-righteousness did for me was create an illusionary life. It was the kind of life that others desired, but really was a shiny plasticized façade that took tremendous energy to maintain.

As I continued to trek down the mountain, I took off the belt of illusion and let go of ever trying to pretend to be someone I wasn't. To be honest, when I was trying to self-validate myself, even with my pastoral peers, it was exhausting. It took a lot of continual energy to please other people because others will never be satisfied. Ugh. I was tired of trying to live that way for decades. No more! I was now a dearly loved son of the King, so what else mattered?

There were other pieces of the rusty armor of self-protectionism that I was able to drop down my mountain hike, but perhaps the two greatest pieces I dropped were the shield of shame and the sword of pride. I began to hike with a lighter step. My body physically felt differently as I dropped years of metal holding me down.

I kept thinking of how it had all gone so very wrong. On the outside, the shield of shame really looked like a shield of faith. How did that turn into something I thought was more important than the God I had professed to worship?

Each step I took down the mountain created new thoughts. I realized that when I experienced difficult situations, I would say I trusted God, and then would use my own energy to make the thing happen. So I said it was my "faith" making it happen. But really my faith wasn't about a trust that God loved me and would take care of me. It was a trust in myself to make things happen. It was a faith in my own beliefs, a belief that I could meet my needs in my own way.

The opposite side of that faith shield was doubt. I doubted that I was worthy of even being loved enough to be cared for by God. That doubt was driven by the deep shame and rejection I felt. The shame was powerful, making me feel like that dirty little boy again. I also experienced shame from my own failures, especially when it seemed that even as a Christian, I still did the wrong things, over and over and over. I came to the sad resolution that I was unworthy of being loved, and I doubted that God would want to help me.

I was breathing easier. At that moment, I let the shield of shame go. I was beginning to experience what it meant to be a dearly loved son of the King. My own efforts had just about destroyed me. So this new journey was going to be trusting in my Creator and King's efforts, not my own. I was ready to drop the sword of pride.

Okay, gut-level honesty time here. How arrogant I was to think I could ever meet my needs my way and be successful at it, but I did.

It always makes me cringe when I say this, but meeting my needs my way was me being god of my own life. The funny thing was, when I looked back over my life, meeting my needs my way never worked. I didn't have great relationships because my self-protection was just that—about self.

Self-protection shuts people out of your life. It did mine. And so my relationships were one-sided, with other people being authentic and me being a hollow shell of a man hiding behind the façade I built.

It also produced poor results at work. Sure, I would meet goals and deadlines at work, but even in ministry, it was often at the cost of dishonoring another person and overriding their thoughts, their feelings, and ultimately their ownership of the task.

This inevitably hurt the organization I was leading.

My "meeting my own needs my way" efforts were arrogance masqueraded as good deeds. This was my sword of pride, a sword that I would swing at anything I thought I should control.

But there was no life in it. It only hurt people. It only hurt me. I saw my arrogance now, and I was so happy to leave this sword along the trail of my hike. I was light now. I was feeling a little vulnerable. But I was free.

As I entered the African plain, the cool breeze flowed down the mountain, refreshing me on my long journey. I hadn't noticed this path before when we were climbing up the mountain. I was wondering if our mountain guide had taken us on another path down, but no matter. It was beautiful, I was on a path, and I felt peace.

Towards the end of the path I was traveling, I saw the most magnificent tree I had ever seen before. It was tall and majestic, with all sorts of animals underneath, zebras, antelope, and monkeys, eating its life-giving fruit. By the tree was a river that gave life to the land around.

As I drew near the tree, I noticed a person. As I got closer, I noticed he was very tall and stately. This wasn't just any person coming towards me; this was the King. He ran to me, and I was scared. I had hidden so much from him, trying to live my life my own way. But he picked up speed until he reached me, gave me a huge hug, and lifted me off the ground. He said, "Welcome home, my son. Now the real journey begins."

You are not the sum of your failures. Your worth is the value of your Creator. Live in his embrace daily.

—VINCENT NELSON

Chapter 4

THE JOURNEY OF BELONGING

I was physically exhausted from seven days on Kilimanjaro and my trip down the mountain, and emotionally exhausted from having lived a lifetime of building a persona that everyone else would accept and love. Really, I was exhausted from building a persona that I would love.

The river running before me, by the magnificent Tree of Life, looked so refreshing. My soul felt as dehydrated and parched as my body. I was tired and could barely move. The physical exhaustion from the hike had caught up, and I had to sit under the Tree and just rest.

I wondered for a second how much farther Bethany was up the trail, but then my mind went back to Alan. How could I ever have a significant life like he did? After everything I'd done, was it even possible?

Just then a voice behind me said, "You're looking mighty serious there."

"What?" I didn't know who it was. I turned around to see the biggest smile before me with the warmest eyes.

"You looked tired and thirsty. Might I suggest you stop thinking for a while and just jump in!" He gave me a friendly slap on the back. "Just follow my lead." Then, without a care in the world, he ran and jumped into the river.

Why not? I said to myself and followed him with a big splash, the kind a kid-sized cannonball makes in a pool.

"Wow, this is so refreshing," I said to the stranger. Only, as I looked at him, he really wasn't a stranger. He looked very familiar. "I'm sorry, I was just talking to the King but didn't notice you. Who are you?" I asked, a little embarrassed, knowing that I probably knew him.

With a deep laugh, he said, "You know me, but don't be hard on yourself. You're seeing me in a different light than you have in the past. I am the firstborn Son of the King!"

I wanted to bow down, but I would have done a face plant in the water. I felt awkward. Almost naked. Here was the King's Son, and I was talking to him. Thousands of thoughts flashed through my mind. I realized this was the Son of the King I had always tried to follow, the one I had known was important and the ultimate example of all that was good, only I never imagined him looking like this.

He wasn't just the firstborn Son of the King, who inherits all power, all authority, and everything that his Father owns. I now saw him as someone who was a friend, the kind of person I would want to climb mountains with.

Seeing him now, I knew I could trust him with the deepest secrets of my soul, the kind of secrets a person might be willing to confide in a best friend, once in a lifetime.

"You look refreshed now," said the King's Son. "Let's get out, dry off, and go for a hike. I have a lot to share, and you're ready to receive."

I noticed he was right. Not only did my body have all its

strength back and then some, but my soul felt alive, relaxed, and rested. I breathed in this moment of peace and climbed out to get ready for our hike.

We began hiking along the river and walked for a while before the King's Son said a word. He was just smiling and whistling, and glanced over at me with a friendly wink when he noticed me looking at him. I felt awkward at times because I wanted to follow him, walking behind him, but every time I tried, he slowed down to walk beside me.

One time during the journey, he even put his arm around my neck, giving me a big brotherly kind of hug, and said, "Vincent, just relax. I don't want you to walk behind me like you're not worthy to be with me. I know you're not going to walk ahead of me. You'd lived life alone, on your own terms, and I know you know how lonely and miserable that was. I want you to walk beside me, right next to me. I want to have a conversation with you."

My soul was hungry for this kind of friendship, so I did as he asked.

"Do you know how much my Father loves me?" said the King's son.

"I'm not sure. I assume a lot."

"Do you remember the time when your son Nick was a baby and fell down the stairs?"

Oh boy, did I. He was just about eighteen months, his mother had run some errands, and I was left with baby duty. We had a baby gate at the top of the stairs to keep him from getting into the bedrooms. I was in the other room when I heard a thud and what sounded like the baby gate hitting the wooden floor at the bottom of the stairs.

I wondered what that noise was since I didn't hear Nick cry. I went in to look and saw Nick, who looked up at me from the floor, blood covering his face, sitting in a small pool of blood. I was in shock. Apparently, Nick decided to climb over the gate, dislodging it, and turned it into his own personal bobsled, seeing if he could ride it down the stairwell for the Olympic gold medal.

My heart raced, and I went into action. I grabbed him and the car keys, then put him in the baby seat and literally drove over a hundred miles an hour to the hospital, not waiting for lights or caring if a police officer tried to pull me over. If they did, they'd just have to give me a ticket after I got there.

I arrived, ran straight in, and demanded immediate treatment for my son. The nurse was irritating. "Sir, please fill out this paperwork, then we'll see him," she said. To which I said, "This is my son, you WILL see him now!"

"Oh ya! Boy, do I remember," I said to the son of the King.

"There's nothing you wouldn't do for your son. There's still nothing you wouldn't do for him, is there?" he asked. "That's how much my Father loves me, and even more. He loves me for who I am."

Wow. I wondered what that kind of love really felt like. The depth of my soul was hungry for that, but it seemed so foreign to me.

I knew my dad loved me, I had seen it. Same with my mom. But there were still times when I felt like I had to be a certain way to be accepted by them truly. Even if that weren't true, that's how I still felt. And as for the King...if the King really knew how dark my heart had been, he wouldn't love me. If the Son of the King knew, he wouldn't be talking to me now. There's just no way.

We walked in silence for a while.

For a short bit, I felt ashamed.

Ashamed for the affair, the lies, getting a DWI after the separation, the addictions and attempts to self-medicate the pain in my soul. But as we continued to walk, seeing the King's Son smile at me, as if knowing every dark thought I had but extending kindness to me through his eyes, I knew it was safe to listen. I didn't have to run anymore.

The King's Son began to share about how he and his Father shared everything—their thoughts, their concerns, even their struggles.

As I listened to the Son, I realized his Dad really loved him. It wasn't just a bunch of meaningless words. The Father was passionate about his Son. They shared their frustrations and their hurts. They laughed together and cried together. And it wasn't just about encouragement. They served each other, putting each other's desires above their own. It was a loyal love.

A love that honored the other. Everything that could be known about the Son, the Father knew. Everything that could be known about the Father, the Son knew. And there was no fear in their relationship. It was the purest form of intimacy I'd ever seen.

"You know, Vince, one of the most meaningful things the King ever said to me, before I had ever done anything significant in this world, was these words for everyone to hear: 'This is my dearly loved Son, who brings me great joy.'

"My spirit soared that day as the King's words embraced me. I was loved simply because of who I am. I'm the dearly loved Son of the King. I was also loved because of whose I am. I belong to and exist because of the King, who happens to be my Dad. I love that, Vince! He embraces me as I am."

We continued walking back towards the Tree without talking for a while. I was thinking about all the Son said. I was thinking about all the failure and selfishness in my life. I could understand why the King would love his Son. His Son was lovable. I, on the other hand, was quite unlovely.

The Son looked at me, smiling as if reading my mind. "Why are you so sad, Vince?"

I stopped dead in my tracks and looked away. "Because I long for what you have, to be known and fully loved and accepted," I said. "To be embraced and encouraged and never be alone. I've spent much of my life scared. I knew of the King, and I've tried to follow your ways: not being selfish and putting others above yourself. I've tried being courageous and choosing what's right above what's wrong.

"I meant well, and wanted to have real friendships, but because I had been hurt by so many, all I knew how to do was try to protect myself physically and emotionally. I was afraid of people. That's what I learned as a child. And I see that fear caused me to live life on my own terms.

"Because I didn't trust and did not let my spouse into my thoughts and heart where I could be hurt, I chose to meet my physical and emotional needs through an affair. I bossed people around because I didn't trust them. I now see how selfish my heart has been. The King would never love me like that. How could he?"

I fell to the ground in tears. It was so painful reliving all the decades of hurt I had caused others, and seeing my selfishness and arrogance. I was ashamed. I was afraid of being rejected once again because I had rejected myself. So how could the King possibly ever love me that way?

The Son sat on the ground and embraced me. For hours I just cried, knowing there was nothing I could hide. And the Son...he just cried with me.

"Vince? Look up," he said. "Do you see where you are?"

We were back under the Tree.

"The Tree gets its life from the River," he said. "The Tree doesn't make itself grow. But the soil, the sun, and the River that its roots are in cause it to grow. It doesn't make itself a huge tree. It's the Life around it that causes it to grow. All it does is receive the Life, and then it grows. And as it grows, it produces fruit for others to eat."

"The Tree is like your life," he continued. "You're valuable. Just as you are. You can't make yourself valuable. It's the Life around you that causes you to grow. You're tied to it. It produces Life in you. You can't produce Life by your own effort. Like the Tree, you receive Life from the River. Vince, the King is the River. When you can receive his water, his words, and his presence in your life, you have all you need. It doesn't matter how many times you've screwed up. That's not what determines your value. I do." The Son gently lifted my face and gazed into my eyes. "Vince, I chose you. And because I chose you, you are my brother, and you are a son of the King!"

As I stared into the most passionately loving eyes I had ever seen, I felt a hand on my shoulder. I looked up to see who it was behind me. It was the King.

"Vince," the King said, "I see you. I know all of you. I love you, Son."

And with that, my soul fell into the embrace of my King.

In the stillness of life you will find what really matters.

—BETHANY WILLIAMS AND VINCENT NELSON

Chapter 5

THE KINGDOM TONGUE

After hours of rest, looking up at the thick clouds and feeling the cool breeze caress my face, I got up at the Son's bidding and sat on a cliff ledge overlooking the valley. Far below us, the River flowed beside the Tree.

As the clouds parted, the warm rays of the sun danced on my face. I closed my eyes, their warmth caressing my face as the Son spoke.

"I want to help you by seeing life a different way using a different language, a Kingdom language," he said. "It's a language that uses the same words you're familiar with but whose meaning is very different from what you're used to and even from what you've experienced."

Kingdom language? What is that? Maybe a King James Bible kind of medieval language of "thous" and "thines"?

As if knowing what I was thinking, he laughed and said, "No, it's not like Old English. It's is an ancient language, older than you can possibly fathom.

"Take the word *love* for example. If I say I love you, there's an instant picture that's associated with that word. The word picture is related to the actions that accompanied the word *love* when it was said to you, perhaps by a parent, a friend, a dating or marriage partner, or even a person of authority over you. If you had fond memories when it was said, you feel an openness.

"But if you had a negative experience when it was said, you feel closed off to that person, guarded, and become untrusting."

I knew exactly what he was talking about. I remember when I was a young child being told, "I love you" but being yelled at immediately afterward for spilling my drink. I felt like while I was accepted for a few moments, I was rejected after that for doing something wrong. I remember thinking as a child, *If I don't do the right thing, I'll get in trouble.*

But as an adult looking back, what I really believed, and was conditioned as a child to think, was, *I'll only be loved if I do the right thing. If I do the wrong thing, I will be unlovable.*

There was another time where the word *love* was twisted in ways that should never happen. It happened when a female babysitter sexually abused me. It happened several times, and I remember her saying, "Trust me, I care about you, it's not wrong." Even as a seven-year-old, I knew it was wrong, but I was too afraid to say anything.

I remember feeling violated, dirty, like I had done something wrong. I wanted to hide, from her and from the world. I just wanted to be safe. And so I learned not to trust people, especially when they would use words like "I love you," or "I care about you." I had lived in a prison of shame, isolation, and protectionism from all relationships, even from healthy relationships, for decades.

The King's Son allowed me time to process all of those thoughts while we walked. Despite the painful memories, walking by the river soothed my soul from the pain of the past. Once I relaxed again, he continued.

"When my Father speaks to me, he always speaks in the Kingdom tongue. There was a time that I just started representing him as an ambassador to a foreign country. Even before I did anything in that role, the King's words to everyone around were, 'This is my Son, love of my life, with him I am greatly pleased.' I remember when my Dad said that. I'll never forget it.

"Before I ever did anything in an attempt to win his love and approval, my Dad made it clear: he loved me just for who I was. I didn't have to earn his love. When my Dad said this, it was the word *love* spoken in the Kingdom tongue. It's the opposite way the world defines love. It's a love that gives, not takes. It's a love of belonging, a love that is given to me, just because I'm the King's Son. It's not a love that's earned by anything I could do. If I were never to do another thing for eternity, my Dad would love me just the same."

Silence filled the air as we continued our hike. My heart burst with desire. If I could only experience that kind of love—a love that gives and doesn't take, a love that embraces, not holds me at arm's length until I do the right thing—what would my life look like? I wasn't even sure how to love myself the right way. And I noticed how intimately the Son talked about the King. I mean, I know the King was his Father, but he called the King his Dad, the kind of way children look up to their parents before they've been hurt by the world.

There was a look of complete love towards the King, of trust, adoration, and receptivity. I could tell the Son had the kind of relationship with the King that whatever his Father asked, he would receive and respond to with wholehearted devotion. And he would do it, not to earn anything, but just because he was loved. I was beginning to understand, the Kingdom language was a language of belonging, of being loved because the

Son belonged to the King.

By this time I was growing hungry. I was confused a bit when I looked up at that same time and noticed we were back at the Tree of Life, the same one where I had been embraced by the King. It was as if we went on a long walk but never left it.

The Son grabbed a piece of fruit from the Tree and threw it to me. It was juicy and sweet, and I felt energized. The Son invited me to sit with him and rest against the Tree, watching the river as it flowed by.

"You know, Vince, when my Dad says he loves me, it's not just that he accepts me as I am. Like I mentioned before, his love is a love that gives. It's life giving. Because I am the King's firstborn Son, I have access to all that my Dad owns. I inherit it. But the difference is, the King has already given it to me because everything with the King is relational. He wants to do life with me and enjoy our relationship together.

"Here's the thing about the kingdom you've missed. Most think belonging means I am to give up my rights and my possessions to another. For example, when you get married, all your possessions become the property of the person you marry. Even the way you live your life is supposed to change if you love with a Kingdom love. If you leave your spouse for a work trip, you check in with them, letting them know where you're at because your time is also their time. They care about you and want to know you're safe, so it's loving to let them know where you're at, that you're safe and when you will return.

"So belonging means that you belong to that person. Even your time belongs to that person. That's partly what the word *covenant* means, like a marriage covenant. What you own belongs to them. That's part of what *belonging* means, but not the whole part.

"Where the world misses it is, that the King, who is all-powerful, who owns everything, also belongs to me. He's my Dad. Because I'm his Son, his heart towards me is to give every good thing. He invites me to experience and live out life with him, even to rule as Son of the King, because as much as I belong to my Dad, all of who my Dad is and owns belongs to me.

"Think about it. Because I am his Son, I inherit all his wealth, all his armies and power, all his resources. But it goes way beyond that; I have the King's DNA. It's been true with the many kings and queens England has had. Most didn't get a crown because they were good; they received it because it was their birthright, because of who they belonged to. So because the King is noble, I am noble.

"It's possible I may not act noble, but I still have nobility coursing through my blood because I belong to him. For me, when I realize how good the King is, how much Dad loves me regardless of what I do, simply because I am his Son, my heart wants to love him back. It's then that I naturally live a noble life because that's in my DNA that my Dad gave me. Because I belong to the King, and he belongs to me, I can say all of these things:

"Because he has all resources, I have unlimited provision. Because he is truth, I am truthful. Because he is noble, I am noble. Because he is love, I am love.

"I am lovable. I can give love. I get to experience true intimacy in its purest form. I am fully known and still fully embraced. Because of that, I can fully know and fully embrace the King, my Dad, and embrace others. I desire to receive from him all he has to say and give. He is my life. I am accepted not because of any other reason but because I am a son of the King!"

A cool breeze blew through the Tree's leaves, and warm shimmers of sunlight danced on my face. All he said penetrated the deepest parts of my soul, parts that had been hidden from the world for decades. Those were the parts that family, friends, and even spiritual leaders—and all the knowledge I had gained—were never able to touch, but somehow, his words had found a way into every crevasse of my being. I wanted what the Son had with the King. I wanted that kind of intimacy.

My eyes revealed my longing for that same kind of love, but still, I struggled with going back to seeing love as something different than he had just shown me. I wasn't worthy of that kind of love. But then again, the Son just said it's not about being worthy; it's about belonging.

I panicked. I felt naked and exposed. Could I ever experience that?

That's when he looked me in the eyes, deep into my soul. His gaze penetrated me. I could see he knew me completely, every thought I had, every action I'd done. Then he said these words:

"Vincent, all I have, you now have, because you have me. You belong to me and I belong to you. All I inherit, I give to you. Because I am, you are. You are loved. You are embraced. You are a noble child of the King."

*Removing the mask that you create
and hide behind frees you to truly develop in
the intimate relationships you are seeking.*

—BETHANY WILLIAMS AND VINCENT NELSON

Chapter 6

IDENTITY DETERMINES DESTINY

The corridor seemed to go on forever as I was whisked down the hallway on a gurney, half out of it. The neon ceiling lights seem to flash one after the other as the attendant pushed me towards the ambulance. "Are you okay, buddy?" I heard him say, knowing he probably had seen this a thousand times before.

I was suicidal, strapped down as they took me to the ambulance, and then drove me to the psych ward, where they would have me on suicide watch. On the drive to the hospital, I felt wave after wave of shame, deep regret, and pain. I had been caught in the affair, called out by a friend who said I could either tell my wife or he would.

I wanted to die. For it all to end. My emotional pain was so intense that it felt like my skin was being cut with a razor blade and alcohol poured over it. I wanted it to stop. I wanted it to end.

I was honest about feeling suicidal with my wife. I was fighting for my life for the sake of my boys. My heart even broke more thinking about the pain they would be facing because of my selfishness. They would end up experiencing the very thing that happened to me, that I had vowed would never happen to them—to grow up in two homes as a result of divorce. But I was trying to live and overcome this pain, lest they grow up without a dad.

The unrelenting waves of pain just kept coming. My God, I had destroyed my family. I had lied to the woman I had the affair with and deeply hurt her. Knowledge of the affair would eventually come out in the church I lead. Hundreds of people would be hurt and let down, especially the board and staff that looked to me to lead them. *My God, what have I done?!*

The siren stopped, and we pulled into the hospital. Quickly, they wheeled me to my room, let me off the gurney, and sat down right outside my door to watch me. I tried to notice the room, with its barren cream-colored walls. All that was in it was a bed. But that's all I needed.

As I curled up in a fetal position, my thoughts continued to race. How did I get here? How did I make the stupidest decisions of my life, one that would cause me to hurt everyone around me, to lose everything good in my life? My wife, my kids and their respect, my job, my home as I'd lose income, respect from my peers and those I lead, my friends who would no longer trust me—everything was gone.

For hours, I cried out to God in that room. *Please, God, take it away. Take it away. Take the pain away. It's too much. Forgive me. I'm so sorry.*

I woke up, still sobbing, with a gentle hand on my shoulder and a loving voice saying, "Vince, it's okay. You're okay. I'm here." I opened my eyes, and sitting right next to my sleeping bag was the King's Son.

"Vincent, you're okay. You were having a bad nightmare. You were reliving what happened in the past."

We stepped outside the tent I was sleeping in, then noticed there was a warm fire blazing with two logs to sit on. We walked over and sat down. I noticed the Son's warm smile and deep penetrating eyes that reflected the dancing flames of the campfire. I was still overwhelmed from that nightmare.

"Those memories are still so painful," I said. "I'm still trying to understand why I did all of those horrific things. I never set out to hurt my ex-wife. I cared about her. I never wanted to hurt my boys, my friends, or those I lead. Why did I do all of those hurtful things?"

The Son sighed as if in pain, then looked at me. "Because you didn't believe you were worthy of being loved. In truth, you hurt others because you believed it was okay to hurt yourself. What we believe about ourselves determines how we live.

"Vincent, this may be a little painful as I ask some questions about your past, but it's to help you see some things, to help you see you are free of those things now. You know I love you, right?"

"Yes, I know you care, go ahead and ask."

"Do you remember how you felt after the babysitter sexually abused you?" the Son asked.

"Yes, I do. I felt violated. Like someone had stolen something they shouldn't. And then...then I felt like something must be wrong with me. I felt deep shame, like I was dirty. The kind of dirt that won't wash off. Which then made me feel worthless. Like I wasn't very valuable."

"Were there other times growing up that you felt worthless?" he asked.

"There's certainly many times, yes," I said. "I can remember feeling like if I didn't do chores a certain way, or say certain things, that I wouldn't be accepted. It felt like if I didn't act the part, then I wouldn't be praised."

"What else? What happened over time as you had those painful experiences with people who were supposed to protect you, supposed to love you?" the Son asked.

This was a very painful question because I could see it was leading to why I had the affair. It was even leading to why, even though as a Christian I knew it was God who meets our needs, why I oftentimes played God, trying to meet my needs my way.

I started to tear up a little. "I began not to trust people. I began to believe that if those who were supposed to love me treated me like that, then there was only one person in this whole world who would protect me...ME."

I saw with blazing clarity what had lead me to the point of making so many destructive decisions, decisions that were intended to protect myself, but decisions that began and ended in selfishness.

The Son put his arm around me. "Vincent, I am well pleased with you. The King is pleased with you. We greatly love you. But you weren't loved by yourself. You did the only thing you knew at the time, and that was to protect yourself. You hid your real self from the world because you believed that you were unlovable.

"Sexual abuse is very destructive because it is so closely tied to a person's being. When someone is a victim of sexual abuse, it steals value from that person. And so through that, you learned others could hurt you and devalue you. What we believe about ourselves determines how we will live. You hurt yourself because you didn't see you were incredibly valuable. And you were afraid that if someone saw the real you, they would reject and hurt you.

"And so, over time, what you did as a way to protect yourself was to not reveal who you really were. You played the part you thought others wanted. You thought they wanted you to be successful to have your value validated. You thought you had to be tough so people wouldn't make fun of you as a child.

"You never let anyone all the way in and so you were incredibly lonely, not for weeks or years even, but for decades. Your friends didn't know your greatest fears. You even kept the King at arm's length because you thought to be loved, you had to perform and build huge ministries all around the world. And so it became about *doing* but never *being*."

When he stopped speaking, the silence cut like a knife. Everything he said was true. I didn't value myself. I shut people out, keeping them from knowing the real me. I even shut God out, not wanting to be vulnerable to him. I had been lonely for decades, never being able to experience true intimacy.

True intimacy is being fully known, knowing the other fully, and still being completely embraced, completely accepted. I had lead a life of isolation for decades and was hurting myself because of it.

And the Son was right. I didn't think I was worthy of being loved. And so even when my own actions hurt me, I kept on doing it, because I wasn't worth more. I believed I deserved any amount of pain caused by others and myself.

That distorted my view of love so much that I became selfish and hurt others. Have you ever reflected back on a painful memory in your own life and simply brushed it under the rug because it was too difficult to relive? I had done that for years.

The warmth of the fire was nice. And the Son's warm smile helped me come back to the present moment of total love and acceptance, not to relive my past pain, shame, and regret.

"Vince, let me help you understand this better, not just with your head, but with your heart too. Identity determines purpose and destiny. What we believe about who we are, that we're lovely or aren't loveable, impacts how we live and interact with others. But understanding our identity alone isn't enough. To truly be empowered to live out your incredible destiny, you have to know in your heart not just who you are but also *whose* you are.

"Knowing who I am cannot be fully lived in and walked out until I know who I belong to. Or rather, where I came from, who my family tree is. Whose I am determines who I am. It goes right back to birthright and inheritance.

"Vincent, you're an elephant!"

I was having a hard time grasping what he was saying, but an elephant?

He stared at me, then burst out laughing.

"What do you mean, an elephant?" I asked.

"Think about it this way," he said. "If your dad is an elephant, then you're an elephant. When a baby elephant is raised in captivity, the owners tie a very strong rope around its leg and the other end to a stake in the ground. The baby elephant tries to break free many times but finally gives up as it realizes it's a prisoner and can't break free. Over time, it comes to accept that the rope is stronger than him.

"Now fast-forward a year or two. The elephant is full grown and powerful. Full-grown elephants are unstoppable. They can pull up trees from the ground with deep roots. They can pull massive amounts of weight. But every time a rope is tied to its leg and a small peg in the ground, it believes that it's stuck and can't move beyond the length of the rope." He let those words sink in for a few moments before continuing.

"Vincent, you've just been an adult elephant that didn't realize you were an adult elephant." He looked deep into my eyes and let these next words penetrate my soul.

"Vincent, whose you are is a son of the King. You're DNA comes from the King. Now let me teach you how to live in the freedom of that truth. It's time to break the rope that's tied you down."

Fear of man is the ability to see my minimal potential and circumstances through other people's limited eyesight. Fear of God is the ability to see my potential unleashed, dreams realized, and the unlimited resources I've already been given.

—VINCENT NELSON

Chapter 7

BE THE ELEPHANT

I woke up early to the smell of coffee on the campfire and fresh baked bread. I poked my head out of the tent thinking it would be the Son making breakfast, but I was amazed to see the King, hunched over, busy cooking.

When he noticed me, he gave me the warmest smile and walked towards me with a cup of coffee. After a great big bear hug and a deep laugh, he said, "Drink up! You have a long day ahead."

I was so nervous I didn't know what to say, so I said very little, and he did most of the talking. The breakfast was fantastic. We sat by the campfire, and he shared about how proud he was of the Son.

He talked about many of the adventures they'd gone on together. He spoke wildly about how kind and smart his Son was and all the amazing things he could make with wood. I could tell he genuinely loved the Son. As he was putting more food on my plate, he looked up at me and said, "You know, Vincent, I'm proud of you too."

He caught me off guard with that statement. He already knew everything there was to know about me, all my failures, how selfish I'd been, and how I certainly haven't lived up to my potential.

"You are?" I asked. "Why are you proud of me?"

"Because you're here now, listening to me. You're taking my words to heart. And you know what? I'm proud of you because you're my son too."

With that, he gave me a friendly slap on the back and went to do the dishes. I jumped up to help him, but the King bellowed out, "I got this. Rest a few minutes before your big adventure ahead."

Just then, the Son stepped out from between some trees and entered the campsite. "Today's a big day." He held a rope in his hand. "We're going to climb a steep mountain that has an incredible view."

I grew fatigued when I thought about climbing again, right after hiking Kilimanjaro, where I lost a friend and several other climbing companions who were evacuated out. That mountain kicked my behind.

"Do you trust me, Vincent?" he said.

"Yes, I do. It's just I don't know if I'll have the energy to climb again."

"I got this," he said. "I know the way and am here to help." And with that, he tossed me a long rope and some climbing gear, and off we went.

It didn't take long for us to reach an almost-vertical cliff that went up for what looked like over 1,500 feet.

The Son pointed to a large cave area about 1,000 feet up. "That's where we're going," he said. "Straight up."

I'd done some rock climbing in my days. I even remember when I was doing some free climbing, and my dad thought I was a lunatic for doing so and yelled out a few explosive rants about me leaving a mess at the bottom of the mountain if I fell. But that was a few hundred feet.

But a climb that far was something I'd never done before, and quite honestly, I didn't think I had the strength to attempt it. "I know you're the amazing adventurer," I said. "The King told me all about your adventures. But I'm tired, and honestly, I don't think I have the strength to do this."

"Vincent, trust me. You know I care about you. I won't steer you wrong. I got this. I got you. You won't fall. I'll make sure of it. I'll go before you and show you the way. You'll even have a safety rope tied to you. All you have to do is listen to every word I say and position your feet and hands in every crevasse I point out. You can do this. You're not alone. I'm with you."

Everything he said wasn't very reassuring. I knew my limitations, and they were staring me in the face. But I knew he loved me, and his words calmed me. I'm with you. I knew he would help me, though I wasn't sure how if I began to slip.

But I trusted him. So I put on my harness, attached my karabiners, and put the rope through it. Then I tied the safety rope to my waist, and up I went, with the Son leading the way.

The cracks in the rock were small but big enough to jam my toes into and slip a few fingers in to pull myself up. I was only about ten feet off the ground, but I noticed the Son was a natural.

It was almost like gravity didn't apply to him. He flew up the vertical cliff almost a few feet a second. He even held his body horizontal with just his arms supporting him. "How's it going? You're looking great."

He flashed a reassuring smile. "These next few places where you'll put your fingers and feet are hard to spot, so listen carefully. Stretch far over to the left now, and you'll grab the first one. Then slide your foot over the rock sticking out, and you'll find a place to put your toes in."

It was incredibly unnerving to not be able to see where to position my hands and feet. I looked down and panicked for a second. I realized I was now 300 feet up and there was no way to see how to get down. I was stuck. The only way down was to fall, and that wasn't an option anymore.

"Vincent, trust me. Stretch to the left, and you'll feel the hand holds."

With a deep breath I reached, and sure enough, I felt the holes. I then reached my leg around the rock, found the foot rest, and slowly slid the rest of my body around the large rock jutting out into my gut.

When I made it around the rock, I was stressed. The kind of stress that lumps in your throat, and you can feel your heart beating at full throttle as if your chest were a racetrack.

"Vincent, you're doing great!"

When I looked up, the Son had come back down about twenty feet and was right above me.

"Just slide two more feet to the right, and you'll step on a ledge that's big enough for you to sit on."

And he was right. Ahhh, I could rest. My hands were trembling a little. But I managed to sit down, with legs dangling over the ledge and feeling the cool mountain breeze on my face.

The Son climbed right over me with ease, reached into his backpack, and pulled out a bottle of water and some food. "Drink up and eat. You're doing great, but we still have a ways to go."

I was happy to do as he said. I was hungry. I was tired and needed a whole lot more energy if I was going to make it up this cliff.

"How much farther is it?" I asked.

"Just a little ways farther," he said. "You'll be there soon."

Well, I'd heard that one before. When I was climbing Kilimanjaro, every day the guides would say, "It's not that much farther. Just a little bit and you'll be there." It wasn't until my fiancée called them out at the end of the trip that they admitted it was always twice the distance we thought it was.

"Ahhhh, I've heard that one before," I told him.

To which he laughed and said, "Vincent, why does it matter how much farther it is? I know this mountain like the back of my hand. I'll get you there. When you ask, 'How much longer till we're there?' do you realize you're measuring your circumstance with your own strength? Meaning, what you're actually trying to do is determine if you're going to make it up this cliff with the strength you have. That's you sizing up whether you can make this climb with your own strength and limited experience. You're limiting yourself because you forget I'm with you. I know exactly what to do. I know you. I know what you need."

He was right. I didn't believe I could make this climb. I certainly began to doubt if I could do the rest of the climb since I was shaking.

"Remember, Vincent, you're an elephant. You have all the strength you need, you have all the resources you need, because I'm with you. Let me ask you this. Where did the baby elephant come from?"

"Well, the older elephant of course."

"So then, the baby elephant has the same DNA its parent does. It has its parent's strength, its agility, its capacity for wisdom even. Although, you don't see all of those things when the baby elephant is young. Yet all of those attributes are still present, in its DNA. The older the calf gets, it can begin using those attributes, but only if it recognizes those in itself. If it believes it's powerful, and it is, then it can easy move huge objects.

"The adult elephant in captivity can easily break the rope around its foot, if it believes it can, because that strength already resides within it."

"So are you saying I already have the strength I need to climb this mountain?" I asked.

"You're free now. You see that. You feel that. You haven't always felt that way," he said.

"That's true. It's still kind of painful because I feel like I destroyed my life, my family's life, and the lives of many who looked up to me. But yes, I am free. I know I have worth because I see it, you've helped me see it."

"Yes, and you're finally listening to me and are receiving into your soul all the King and I say about you. And what have we said about you?" the Son asked.

"That the King loves you. There's nothing he wouldn't do for you. You are the most valuable thing to him, above all he has. And that the King says I'm his son too."

"Yes, Vincent, as much as I am the image of the King, you also carry his DNA, his value. When he sees you, he sees my worth."

"But what does this have to do with me being like an elephant?" I asked.

"Because if I have a problem or struggle, the King loves me so much, he'd fight any army to get to me and make sure I have all I need. Within the elephant is the same strength of his parent. It has all it needs to break free of the rope around its ankle. It just gave up and never sought to use its resources because it doubted who it was and who it belonged to, its family of elephants.

"Vince, you're the King's son too, and he'd climb any mountain, cross any sea, fight any army to help you. All of his resources are yours. But the King is relational. If you don't want his help, if you don't ask for his help, even though you have royal blood coursing through your veins, then you'll live life as whatever captive you think you are.

"If you've been hurt early in life, as you have been, then you'll shut out people and learn to rely on only yourself and your limited resources.

"If you're lonely, you won't seek authentic relationships; you'll instead use people to meet your needs of loneliness, trying to fill that void your own way."

The Son was right. That's exactly what I did. It pains me to admit this, but I did use women to fill that void of loneliness in my life, a void I created because I didn't trust people, not even my wife, with the deepest parts of my heart.

So I kept people at arm's length, created loneliness because of it, and then used friendships, relationships, and ultimately the affair to self-medicate my pain. And I realized that cycle of meeting my needs my way created all sorts of addictions, like being a drug user or an alcoholic. I had firsthand experience of being a workaholic to get my value from what I did, or being a gym junkie to try to increase my value by looking better physically.

The Son picked up my train of thought as if he already knew what I was thinking.

"Whether it's being a drug addict, workaholic, or sex addict," he said, "all of those are like a strong rope that was tied to people's ankles when they were younger. They were hurt, just like you, and learned how to rely on themselves and their own limited resources, forgetting they were not designed as a delicate creature, but a mighty force that could break free from their pains and life circumstances. Either they never learned, or they forgot somewhere along the way, that they are children of the King, full of nobility, of purpose, of destiny, having all resources of the King available if they'd only listen to what the King and I say about them."

I was beginning to breathe in deeper than I ever had before. I was still scared as I looked down, straight down. But I was starting to see hope for the future.

"Let's keep climbing," the Son said, and up he went, guiding me every step with my safety rope attached to him.

"You now see that by choosing to meet your own needs your own way, you ended up hurting so many people, including yourself. But do you realize what created the rope around your ankle to begin with?" he asked.

I figured it was the hurt inflicted by others that caused me to hurt others, but I wasn't sure. "I guess I don't know. What created the rope?"

"An inner vow. Early in life, you determined you'd be your ultimate protector, provider, nurturer, teacher. When you said to yourself, *I'll never let anyone hurt me again,* you became the King."

He let that thought sit for a minute, then continued, "You decided that you would be king of your own life. The problem is, you were never meant to replace the King. By yourself, you don't have all the resources to provide for yourself. You alone can't protect yourself from harm.

"You've experienced that firsthand as you destroyed your friendships, your influence, your family, and your career. Worse yet, because you relied on yourself, not listening to the King or anyone else, your perspective of truth became skewed. Your world became all about you. Which meant you began making decisions that you thought benefited yourself but in truth hurt so many others, people who loved you and trusted you. And as you tried to live as your own king, you became an enemy of the King."

"No, there's no way," I said, shaking my head. "I would never try to hurt the King or defy him."

The Son didn't speak. He just let me think about it.

I looked out across the beautiful landscape under my feet, but all I saw was the darkness of my past heart. He was right.

"You're right," I said. "My King, I'm so sorry," I said out loud. "Son of the king, I'm so sorry. I never realized I was trying to be King. Please forgive me," I said in a soft whimper.

"Vincent"—he lifted my head to catch his eyes—"I already

have. The King loves you. He loved you even when you were an enemy of his. But now," he said with a chuckle, "now you're a son of the King! When you receive me, you receive your birthright, who you are and where you come from. And you're listening. You're finally listening and trusting and letting the King's words all the way into your heart.

"Here's a deeper truth, Vincent. You already have everything you'll ever need because you already have the King. If you want to live in the freedom you're experiencing now, then walk with the King. Listen to him. Receive into your heart all he says about you and your value. Learn who the King is and live as the noble son that he's already made you to be."

Wow, that was a lot to take in. The Son let those thoughts just linger with me for a while.

High above, an eagle soared in the brilliant blue sky. White, pink, and purple flowers dotted the green grassy plain, and the Tree of Life next to the river gave life to the valley. I'd never known how beautiful this world was until now, seeing with the eyes of a son, a son of the King.

Just then my right hand slipped, and I lost my grip. Then the small ledge that held both of my feet dislodged and my feet lost their foothold. I looked down. We were about 900 feet up, and our climb was about to end abruptly.

"Help, I'm slipping!" I screamed out.

"Let go, Vincent, I got you," the Son said.

I desperately tried to hang on with my left hand, but it was beginning to cramp.

"Let go, Vincent. Trust my grip and my strength. I'll swing you to the next section. Do you trust me?" he asked.

I took a deep breath. *I'm the elephant. I'm a noble son of the King. The Son loves me. He has me.* And with that, I let go. It felt like the fall lasted minutes, but in truth, it was only a few seconds. My eyes were closed, but I heard the Son say, "Reach up high to the left and grab the ledge."

When I opened my eyes, the ledge was fast approaching. He swung me toward it, and I reached out and grabbed it, then pulled myself up. I couldn't believe my eyes.

In one swing the Son landed me at the very cave entrance we were climbing to. It only took a few minutes for him to join me. The amazing thing was, there was already a fire blazing with food cooking over it. We quickly got our gear off, sat down, and began to eat.

The view was spectacular, even better than before on the lower ledge. I could see the entire Kingdom now, and it was magnificent.

"Well done on the climb, Vincent. When you walk with and listen to the King, you have all you need."

I looked at the Son. "I'm free."

"You're free," he said, "because you're a child of the King. Listen and receive and you'll live in the incredible destiny that awaits."

If I believe I can't walk with God because of my failures, then I'm living as a servant. If I believe I can walk with God even though I have failed, then I'm living as a son.

—VINCENT NELSON

Chapter 8

THE TWO PRINCES

We sat for a while, enjoying the breeze and the beauty of the Kingdom before the Son packed up his gear in a bag.

"How are we going to get down?" I asked. "I thought we'd have to rappel."

"Don't worry. I know the way." Throwing the bag over his shoulder, he proceeded through a small opening into the darker part of the cave.

I quickly loaded up my gear and followed.

The cave was very dark, and the floor was slick, with a slight downward slope. There were a few times I slipped, but every time the Son was there to catch me. It was odd too.

Whenever the Son was farther ahead of me, the cave would grow darker, making it hard to see. Yet the closer he was, the better I could make out the walls around me, even though he didn't carry a light. It was a good thing too because, by that time, we had gone so far down I could no longer see the light from the cave entrance.

We continued our journey, farther and farther downward.

"Vincent, there's a story the King used to tell me that I want to share with you. It's the story of two brothers who were princes and sons of another king.

"The king loved his sons and built his kingdom for his sons to enjoy, knowing that one day they would also have the responsibility of leading the kingdom. So he taught them from an early age how to rule. He taught them the difference between right and wrong, about love and adventure. He would tell them magnificent stories as they went on long hikes together and explored the lands.

"He oftentimes would have the servants teach them, everything from how to read, write, cook, and help harvest the king's grain. The princes also learned how to use a shield and sword, clean the stables, and ride horses. The king wanted them to learn and experience all the goodness he could bring to others. He wanted them to grow as princes who would extend that same kind of goodness to all in the kingdom. The king loved his sons and watched them grow from children into young noblemen.

"Over time, though, the youngest son became restless. He didn't like doing chores with the servant. He thought he was much better than a servant and thought they should wait on him because he was so much more important than them. When his father would help him see that the servants were people with great worth and should be treated as such, he thought his dad was unfair.

"*Father doesn't love me because he doesn't think I'm special, he thought. He wants me to do things that are beneath me, so I'll just do what I want to do,* and with that, the younger prince's heart grew cold and resentful towards the king. His thinking fell even darker: *My older brother is first in line to be king, and this is as good as life will ever get!*

"So he made plans to take half of the gold in the treasury, gold that was his inheritance when his father would one day die. He quickly took the gold and left the castle and his father far behind, exiting for another land far away. He was determined to create his own kingdom, one in which he would rule the way he thought it should be done.

"At first, the younger son loved his new life. He signed a deed, promising to pay for a beautiful castle he purchased. He hired servants to do all his work. He began throwing parties, parties that were bigger than the king had ever thrown. In a short time, he had more friends than he thought possible. Men envied him. Women loved him.

"He spent more and more money throwing parties, not knowing how fast his resources were dwindling. He even invested in a local business but didn't want to concern himself with the work, so he hired managers to run it. And he ruled them with an iron fist, demanding unrealistic returns and ignoring their counsel on how to invest back into the business.

"He thought to himself, *Now, this is what it means to be the king! Something my father doesn't have a clue about.* In the matter of a few months, though, a great famine came to the land he was in. It hadn't rained in months. Crops began to die. Cattle died of thirst.

"He went to his treasury to get more money for supplies, but by this time the parties he threw had wiped out all of his savings. He quickly realized all of his so-called friends were nowhere to be found. His servants quit. His business failed because he didn't invest back into it the way his managers suggested. And finally, he was kicked out of the castle with an unpaid deed.

"Overnight he was broke and worse off than the servants he hired. He had no money and no skills for a job. He had no friends because of the cruel reputation he had developed. No one wanted to help him. The only possessions he now owned were the clothes on his back.

"He began to starve, not having eaten for a week. The only job he could find was working in a stable, shoveling horse manure. When his boss wasn't looking, he'd grab a handful of grain from the horse's trough and shove it into his mouth.

"As he thought about his life, he reflected back to his father. He remembered as a boy his father holding his hand and swinging him in the wheat fields. He remembered long walks with the king, learning lessons about how all people mattered, and it was the king's heart for them to know and experience his goodness, even the servants.

"He thought to himself, *I've hurt my father's heart deeply. I robbed him and stole gold from his treasury. There's no way he would ever allow me to be a prince again. But he's so kind to his servants; maybe he'd at least allow me to be that and be able to experience the good things they do.* Dropping the shovel in his hand, he started the long journey home."

With each step down into the cave, I listened. I wanted to thoroughly understand what the Son was trying to teach me. I could see I was that young prince who had done life on my own terms. I had made myself an enemy to the King, trying to steal his role and rule my life my way.

"So what happened when the young prince finally made it home?" I asked.

"It took a long time for him to make it home, over a month," the Son said. "Meanwhile, though, as the younger son went off to create his own kingdom, the older prince was hard at work, taking care of his father's kingdom.

"The older son grew up with the servants, doing what they did, with all the chores of the kingdom. The older prince had the same walks with his father, having fun and going on adventures. But somewhere over time, the older prince became so concerned with the details of the kingdom that he was as diligent as the servants in their work. He thought, *I bet my father is proud of me for cleaning the stable. If I do more than the ser-vants who are working on the harvest, he'll be even more happy with me.*

"As the older son grew into a young man, he was very responsible. He was now over all of the servants, directing them, making plans to grow the king's business and use that money to buy more land and expand the kingdom.

"He thought to himself, *I have done so much, I know the king is pleased with me. I bet a lot more than my do-nothing younger brother. I know he has to love me more than him.*"

By this time in the story, my legs were growing tired. The Son caught me for the tenth time, so we sat on a big rock in the cave, and he asked a question. "So which son do you think the king loves more?"

"Well, I'm suspecting the older son, who did all his father asked," I said.

"We shall see," the Son said. "About the same time that the older prince was becoming so successful, the younger son was almost home. The king had done what he always did every day since the younger prince left. Every day he walked the lands in the afternoon, the same paths he had walked with his two boys when they were children. He hoped against all hope that he would one day see his younger boy again.

"One early evening when he was walking alone, a servant came to let him know they spotted his younger son miles away, heading towards home. The king, before the servant was done talking, took off running as fast as he could in the direction the servant told him to go. He ran for miles until he finally could see his son and then picked up speed.

"The younger son was slowly walking towards the castle, hoping against all hope that his father would allow him to return and live with the servants. He wondered how angry his father would be for taking the gold and if he'd be allowed even to enter the kingdom.

"And then he saw his father, with robes blowing in the wind, running the fastest he had ever seen. His father was coming right for him. *He doesn't want me here. He's coming to punish me. I deserve it, though. I deserve whatever he decides to do,* he thought. When the king was only a few yards away, the son fell to the ground and in tears yelled out, 'Please forgive me.'

"Just then the king opened his arms wide, leaned down, grabbed him with the strength of a bear, and picked him up. Laughing and crying huge tears of joy, he said, 'My son, you're finally home.'

"The servants had finally caught up to the king. The king told them to throw the biggest party the world had ever seen. 'Spare no expense,' he said. 'My son, the prince, has finally returned home.'

"It was the most extravagant party the younger prince had ever seen. All the people of the kingdom were there, celebrating his return. Each of the servants he had been unkind to before now showered him with kindness.

"The younger son realized he was finally home and understood what it meant just to be, be loved on by his dad, and just be the son of the king. His rebellious actions towards the king didn't unmake him a son. And he finally began to live as the prince he had been born to be, leading with kindness, staying humble, and wanting to be responsible out of love for his dad, the king.

"When the older prince heard about the party, he refused to join them. A servant told the king this, and he went outside to invite the older prince to come in to the celebration. 'My son, your brother has returned. His heart has returned home. Don't you want to welcome your brother home?' the king asked.

"'Are you kidding?' the older prince said. 'You're going to welcome this good-for-nothing son of yours home? Really? You're going to welcome him back home after stealing half of the treasury, after being incredibly arrogant and thinking work was beneath him? I've spent decades working for you. I've worked just as hard as your servants, harder even, and yet not one time have you ever thrown a party like that for me. I'm done. I obviously can't do enough to make you proud of me.'

"In tears, the king said to his older son, 'Your brother has returned. He was lost, but now he's found. His heart was dead to us, but now it's open and alive. He's finally home.'"

The Son got up and started walking down the cave floor. I followed close behind and the light was getting brighter. In a few moments, we turned a corner and were outside again, on top of a small hill at the bottom of the steep cliff. The brilliance of the sun was blinding, causing me to take a few moments to regain clarity of the horizon, but it was warm and my body drunk in its heat.

I didn't realize how cold the cave was until the chill on my bones began to melt away. Between the tall green pine trees, I could see the golden valley below. I breathed in the sweetness of the fresh air and the sweet scent of the trees. The daylight welcomed me, and I felt peace. This is what it must have felt like to the younger prince to finally be home.

We continued our walk to the Tree.

"So, which son do you think the king loved more?" the Son asked.

I thought about it for a minute. "I know the younger son finally returned home, but the older son always did the right thing. He always did what his father asked. So I'd still probably say the older prince."

"Actually, he loved them both equally deeply and passionately, because they both belonged to him," he said. "So the next question is, who do you think made the better prince?"

"Well, that's easy," I said. "It's the older, more responsible one."

"Actually, no. It's the younger one," the Son said.

"What? Why is that?"

"Notice that the younger son finally listened to his dad. He received his love. He saw that his dad didn't love him for the things he did or didn't do. He loved him simply because of who he was and who he belonged to as a son of the king. The younger prince finally had an open and listening heart towards the king. He was able to lead from the security of his dad's love for him. He finally had nothing to prove.

"Proving is about measuring. In the case of the princes, they were trying to prove they mattered; they had value. The younger prince tried to do that by becoming more than he thought he was in his own mind. That way of thinking is a crazy maker; you can never do enough to increase your worth because you can never know where the target really is. You'll never arrive and find peace. Only after messing up did the young prince finally understand that if he stopped trying or if he messed up, he still was loved and valued by his dad, the king. The young prince finally saw his value was found in his dad's love for him, and how greatly loved he was.

"Because of that, the prince would lead from a place of love. He would go on to rule as a prince who had nothing to prove, no value to be gained by anything he did. He simply wanted to make a difference in his dad's kingdom for the betterment of others. He was finally able to lead the kingdom the same way his dad did, from a place of security and love. That's when the young prince could finally lead the kingdom with honor and nobility.

"Now think about the older son. He lived life trying to find value and approval by doing more. He was trying to prove his worth. He believed that he had to perform in order to win his father's love.

"The older son's own words reveal that he doesn't live like a son, but as a servant, when he said, 'I've worked just as hard as your servant, harder even.' He doesn't see himself as a dearly loved son; he sees himself as someone who has to earn his status, like a servant earns their wages. In truth, Vince, because the older son believed that about himself, he treated everyone around him the same way."

As soon as the Son said this, my heart sunk. How many times as a pastor had I worked hard to build ministries all around the world, thinking that I would be valuable, that if I did enough of the right things, it would outweigh the dark things in my heart? I realized that I honestly believed that if I did enough for the King, he would finally accept me. I also realized I had treated others the same. They needed to work as hard as I did, to measure up. How exhausting and lifeless that was.

I knew better, but because I allowed the pain of my past to separate me from relationships, thinking I had to take care of myself and look out for me, I put distance between the King and me. And because of that, I was unable to receive from him. I believed I was the only one who could take care of me. And the sad thing was, even as a pastor knowing that was a wrong thought, my heart still believed it. How miserable, tiring, and destructive did that belief turn out to be for me!

"I can't believe how many times I was openly rebelling against the King, calling myself king of my own life," I said. I never outright said I was king of my own life, but my actions revealed that I believed it.

The Son just looked at me and smiled. "So you see now that when we try to be king, we find our resources are limited for meeting our own needs. And our perspective of life is narrow; we think we're doing well when in fact we're being self-centered and making it about ourselves. But the moment we can truly see ourselves as a son of the King, when we receive his love, listen to him, and follow him, then we find we have all we will ever need.

"You're a son of the King, Vincent. He's your Dad. You don't have to earn his love. You don't have to prove anything to me, yourself, or anyone that you are a son of the King. But choosing to listen and receive from the King all of who he is and all of what he says allows you to live as the incredible prince he's made you to be.

"But to be a prince, you first have to be a son. To be a great leader, you first have to see that you belong to the most excellent leader. Before you ever do, just be. Be the dearly beloved son of the King you are. And as you grow in maturity through listening, you'll grow into the magnificent prince that your noble heritage and destiny declare."

As we headed down from the mountains into the valley, I could again see the Tree by the River far off in the distance.

We spent the rest of the time walking in silence. Not an awkward silence, but one that gave me a deeper sense of belonging, of value in my soul. I was loved not for what I have done, haven't done, or will ever do. I was loved simply because I was a son of the King.

A tremendous sense of destiny and purpose filled my heart. I didn't know what it was, but I knew that I belonged to the greatest king that has ever existed. And I wasn't just a son; I was noble, I was a prince because within me lay the King's DNA, the King who governs the galaxies and the cosmos. The King who holds atoms together and builds stars. I was a child of the King.

*What if we no longer measured others by who we were,
threw away the measuring tape and
loved people into their destinies?*

—Vincent Nelson

Chapter 9

A TALE OF TWO KINGDOMS

"Today we get to see another Kingdom," said the Son.

I opened my eyes.

He was standing outside my tent. "We're going on a long hike. Are you ready to see a place that's familiar yet different?"

Familiar yet different? That was an interesting way to wake up. I quickly got ready, had breakfast, and put on my backpack, eager to see what this riddle held in store.

We set off, and once we got past the plains with the River and the Tree behind us, we began descending rapidly.

"I thought we were already in the valley," I said. "I had already come off the mountain summit."

The Son smiled. "We're going into the lowlands today. Vince, there are two types of places. There's the highlands where the nobles live, children of the King. Then there are the lowlands, where the children of the World's Kingdom live.

"The children of the King, which you're one of, have the

ability to see both the heights of our King's Kingdom and see the valley of the World's Kingdom. They, like you, have the capacity to see all of life with the King's perspective. Then there are the people of the lowlands; these people only have the capability to see what's in front of them. Their perspective is limited to the world around them."

"So we're going to a different place that's a kingdom?" I asked.

"Yes and no," the Son said. "We are hiking into a town today, but even though it's the lowlands, you'll still see two different kingdoms existing, side by side. The Kingdom of heaven, our Dad's Kingdom, isn't fixed to a location. It's everywhere He is. And because you're his son, it's everywhere you are. It's everywhere the King's children live."

We continued our downward descent, crossing rivers and seeing all sorts of trees and wildlife. As we cleared the tree line, I could see a deeper valley below. We continued down a path into the lowland town.

"So I've been thinking about what you said," I began, "but I'm still a little confused. I know the King. I know he's good. I know he's the leader of my life and I have everything I need in him. He's my provider. But what is his Kingdom in reality all about?"

"You know what the Kingdom is, Vincent, because you know our King and you know me. It's all the King's goodness extended to all around.

"Think about what his goodness is. It's his love. His honor. His nobility. His provision. His peace. His healing. His hope. His justice. His kindness. His embrace. So when people experience the King, they experience his Kingdom, an extension of himself. Where the King is, there is freedom to experience and live in his goodness.

"Vincent, you as his child carry his DNA, so you extend his goodness just by being the child he's already made you to be.

Think about the Kingdom this way. When you breathe in his goodness, you exhale his goodness to the world around you. It's as simple as breathing. Receive it in, and then release it to others. That's what the Kingdom is like."

As we walked into town that morning, I noticed it was busy. Cars moving quickly. Parents taking kids to school. One of those cars almost ran over a kid crossing the street to get there.

"Watch out!" I yelled, but the little girl crossing the street didn't hear me. Fortunately, the car skidded to a stop before it hit her.

"Oh, I forgot to tell you, they can't hear or see you. Today we're just observing. Think of yourself as a type of Scrooge, just without the attitude readjustment, though you may get that too." The Son laughed.

As we continued walking, I noticed an old beggar, probably in his eighties, on the street. It looked like he was paralyzed from the waist down based on the way he was sitting on the mat. He held a big sign in his lap that read, "Homeless and hungry, need help." There were a few people who passed him by and didn't pay any attention until he yelled at them, begging for money. And they would throw spare change at him.

Then another slightly younger man, probably in his sixties, stopped, looked the beggar square in the eyes, and asked, "What's your name?"

The old beggar said his name was Ralph.

"Well, Ralph, nice to meet you. I'm Tom," the other man said. "I've noticed you've been on this street corner for many years. Have you ever tried to get help?'

"I ask for money all the time, but no one ever gives me enough."

"I don't have any money, but what I do have, I'll give to you." With that, Tom waved at some guys, who brought over a brand-new wheelchair. "I have a wheelchair as a gift for you, to be able to get around. Come with me to the shelter where I have some food, fresh clothes, and a bed waiting for you."

Tom looked deeply into Ralph's eyes and said, "Ralph, you are loved. You have value. And today I want you to see that. I have a story to tell you about a King and his goodness for you." And with that Tom hugged Ralph for a moment, lifted him into the wheelchair, and took him to the shelter.

"Wow," I said to the Son. "That younger guy was so nice."

"Tom isn't younger than Ralph. Tom is eighty-two. Ralph is sixty-eight. But you're right about Tom. Tom is from the highlands; Ralph is from the lowlands. Tom is a son of the King. Ralph doesn't know the King.

"The interesting thing is, Tom doesn't have any more material possessions than Ralph does. Tom lives at and runs the shelter. Tom doesn't have a big bank account or a generous retirement plan. He simply knows that he's a son of the King. And as a son of the King, he has everything he needs. Even though it looks like he doesn't have anything, he has everything. Tom raised some money to get a wheelchair for Ralph.

"Tom organized the guys to go help get Ralph. And Tom is spending time with Ralph to help him see that he matters. Ralph has had a hard life and has lost much, including his family. But today Tom is going to help Ralph see that he *does* have a family, a royal family. Ralph will see that he doesn't have to beg for money. That he has everything he needs and more to give away.

I nodded. "I think I understand what you're saying. These are bold statements, but would these thoughts sum up what it looks like to be a son of the King? Maybe something like...

Because the King is loving
I am loved
I love others

Because the King is noble
I am noble
I help others see their value

Because the King is courageous
I am courageous
I help others overcome adversity

Because the King is rich
I have endless resources
I freely give to others

Because the King is peace
I am peaceful
I extend peace, not strife, to others

"Is that what the Kingdom looks like?" I asked.

The Son stopped and laughed, then slapped me on the back. "You're definitely getting it. You see life with Kingdom eyes. Now let's go see what both kingdoms really look like in people's lives. You saw in Tom how rich his life was, even towards the end of it," he said. "But I want you to see what the Kingdom looks like right in the middle of life when most people haven't yet gained perspective of what's paramount in life."

The Son led me into what appeared to be the typical suburban home, with a husband, wife, and two kids. At first glance, it seemed like a happy family. Then I noticed the husband appeared to be self-absorbed, working on a spreadsheet on his computer. His wife began yelling at him, calling him useless because he never helped with the kids, especially in the morning when it was hard to get them ready in time for the bus.

She was yelling about an annual report she had to prepare for her job, that she was behind and needed more time to complete it before her 9 a.m. meeting. Looking stressed and frustrated, she got the kids on the bus, slammed the door to the house without saying good-bye to her husband, and sped out of her neighborhood.

The Son turned to me. "So, Vince, what Kingdom is this couple living in?"

"Looks like the average stress-filled American family to me," I joked. "The husband's preoccupied with his own life. I've lived that before, which in truth is a selfish life. The husband is masquerading as the 'provider of the family.' When I was like that, it was primarily about making myself feel valuable and needed.

"When my wife asked for help, I decided what I was doing was more valuable than helping her. I was doing good, so I thought. In my mind I was doing the nobler thing, taking care of my family, though I was missing what was most important to everyone in my family. I feel pain from watching that and remembering how selfish I was. So for the husband, I would say he's living in the World's Kingdom.

"That's true," the Son said. "What about his wife, Paula?"

"Well, the ironic thing is, I've been her too. I remember asking for help and being mad because it didn't happen when I wanted it nor the way I wanted. So if I didn't deal with that anger by trying to release it, I grew resentful. It killed intimacy between my spouse and me, and it made me not want to help her or be with her. I felt like I didn't matter to her and so I tried to find other ways to self-medicate my feelings to find value, and that was very destructive. I was trying to live my life my way. Which I guess isn't the King's Kingdom, because it was about my own kingdom. It was selfish."

"Very insightful," he said. "So you can easily spot what the World's Kingdom looks like. Let's see what the King's Kingdom looks like."

As we walked into an local business, I noticed an older boss was leading a small team of folks. The team was reporting on the different cities they did marketing in. The Chicago team leader happened to be Paula, whom I saw earlier. She shared her report and had a PowerPoint slide show showing a decline in revenues in that market. Paula's boss verbally attacked her as soon as she shared that, saying what a useless marketing expert she was.

The boss didn't try to understand what was going on in Chicago; he instead spent that time trying to intimidate the rest of the team by calling them stupid and lazy, in an effort to get them to produce more. The marketing person from New York, Peter, spoke up and praised Paula for helping to open new leads for him in his market. Peter's boss laid into him, chastising him for not doing his own job.

After the meeting was over, Peter went over to encourage Paula, then went into his boss's office and closed the door.

"Boss, why are you belittling Paula for helping me? That's just not right. What's going on in your life? Is there something you're struggling with that we can really help you with?"

The Son turned to me "So, Vince, what about here?"

"Well," I said, "the boss definitely is of the World's Kingdom."

"Yes, but don't focus on the World's Kingdom. Tell me, where you see the King's Kingdom?"

"I think it's the New York marketing executive, Peter. Not only did he reach out to encourage Paula, but he stood up for her. He showed courage, not once, but twice when he went into his boss's office to tell him that was wrong for belittling Paula. And Peter showed a lot of nobility because he respected his boss and didn't humiliate him in front of Peter's peers when he corrected him. Then Peter went one step further by reaching out to his boss to help by asking about the deeper issues causing his boss's frustration."

"That's true. And do you know why the New York executive did those things?" the Son asked.

"Well, it took some significant courage to walk into his boss's office and be willing to correct him. He must have been very secure in who he was, enough to not care what his boss thought about him. He must have seen his worth and value within."

"You see it now," the Son said. "The Kingdom isn't about being good enough or doing good things. It's not about being good. It's not about not doing bad things, the avoidance of evil. It's about simply belonging to the King. Being a child of the King comes with an awareness of who the King is and how much you are dearly loved and valued by him.

"As you receive that, you can't help but extend that to others. In this case, Peter helped others feel valued and loved, and displayed courage in the face of adversity. Like so many who have gone before you, names you'll know. Dr. Martin Luther King, who knew he wasn't the ruler of his own life, but knew he was a son of the King, bowed his will to the King, and experienced the King's goodness for himself. Because he listened to the King and experienced his goodness, he couldn't stand the injustice and hatred of this World's Kingdom. He fought the hatred of this World's Kingdom with the weapons of peace, courage, and love.

"As a noble son of the King, he used those weapons to bring the King's goodness to a nation. Or how about Abraham Lincoln, who as a believer understood all people regardless of their skin color, to have inalienable rights given by the King. He couldn't help but lead the way his Dad and King lead because he was a child of the King."

The Son took some time to let all of that sink in as we walked outside to a park close by. We sat down on a bench, right by a children's play area with sand. As I looked at the children playing, I noticed the Son drawing circles and words in the circle. The first one had these words:

"Vincent, do you see these children playing? Look how happy and carefree they are. Why is it that as they get older in life, the dreams they have of being anything they want to be fade away?

"Why is it that many of them lose the smiles on their faces and seem to just grin and bear life as they become older adults? Do children naturally set out to hurt each other and become murders, cheat on their spouses, or stop dreaming big dreams? Of course not.

"Children start out as blank canvases to paint huge dreams on. They are happy; they are the princes and princesses of their own magnificent stories. But somewhere along the line they get hurt and disappointed by others; they fail one too many times and give up. Life starts to steal their joy, and they become the average adults that you see all around you, the adult that you used to be. They live life from a selfish perspective. And they eventually settle for living in the World's Kingdom, a world of self-striving, of mediocre dreams, of pain, of 'as good as it will get' jobs and relationships.

"Vincent, when you were first born, you saw the world in the purest way. But as you grew up, your experiences, your pain, what you experienced with your parents, what religion taught you, and things the world taught you, like, 'Looking out for number one will get you ahead,' all shaped how you see the world around you. These experiences were like glasses, lenses that would shape how you saw yourself, what you believed about others, and they ultimately impacted your decisions and behavior."

He pointed to the first circle he drew. "Those lenses are our worldview, and they determine what we believe to be true, what we believe is good, which affects our decisions and actions. For example, do you remember when you were young and you vowed you'd never let anyone hurt you again?

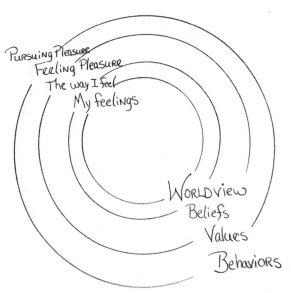

"At that moment, you determined that you alone were the only one who would care for and look after you. Neither the King, your parents, nor anyone else was able to take care of you. That is what you experienced and believed.

"And so it became about your feelings, like this circle. You believed you couldn't trust anyone and wouldn't find what you needed by being vulnerable. So to meet you emotional need for intimacy, you said in your own mind, *I want to feel loved, I want to feel valued.*

"So you would seek out relationships with others who needed you, who would depend on you, only to make yourself feel more important. And so you lived life, even as a pastor, not living in the King's Kingdom, but instead in the World's Kingdom because it was never about the King. All the 'good things' you were doing in the church didn't occur because you were the King's dearly loved child; they were done to make you feel more important.

"Vince, I'm not sharing this to make you feel bad; it's to show you what the two Kingdoms look like in a person's soul and how it affects how they live and impact others' lives."

"No, I understand. I get it," I said. "I wasn't living as a child of the King. Even as a pastor I was living as a child of the World's Kingdom. It was never about me just belonging; it was about me doing and striving. My life wasn't about the King; it was about me. And in so doing, I was missing real freedom for my life. Freedom to be who the King created me to be. I lived life as a human *doing*, not as a human *being*.

"I see what the two kingdoms look like, but how do I help others move from World's Kingdom to the King's Kingdom?" I asked.

"It's easier than you think, Vince." The Son smiled. "Live life as the noble child of the King you already are. He is with you. And so you also have all he has.

"You have the words you need to encourage people, the patience you need to show love in the midst of hurtful actions that affect you. You have the courage you need to confront injustice in the world.

"You have the strength to confront the deeper issues a

friend might be dealing with, with the affair they are having. You see the behavior of the affair is a symptom a deeper issue, maybe a deep hurt, causing them to try to meet their needs their own way rather than being honest with themselves about how they are feeling, and talking it out with their spouse. You see, that deep thing that is driving their behavior and can speak love, kindness, courage, and freedom to it. It's love and kindness that lead people to the King. It's freedom they are searching for.

"You also understand that it's ultimately connecting them with the King, where they move from the World's Kingdom into the Kingdom of heaven, where they will live as free men and women, filled with courage, living as the nobles they were created to be, living lives that fulfill dreams and massive destinies.

"And Vincent, you do all these things with the uniqueness of who you are, with your unique experiences, talents, and skills. When you live as a child of the King, you bring the King with you, into those people's lives. See the world around you through the King's eyes, with the priceless value he sees in others. Help them see themselves the way the King does. For where you are, the King's Kingdom is."

If the negative words of others or even yourself discourage you from pursuing your dreams, don't give up! You are loved, you are worthy, you are a dearly loved child of the King!

—VINCENT NELSON

Chapter 10

AN INTIMATE WALK
WITH THE KING

It was dark. I could barely see, but thanks to the help of the usher with a flashlight, I was able to maneuver around the curtains that blocked all light. I could hear lively music, though, coming from on stage. And the people's cheers were almost as loud as the band.

"Right this way, Mr. Nelson," said the usher as he escorted me backstage. "As soon as the band is done, you'll walk out and take center stage."

From backstage, I could see the crowd. It wasn't just a few hundred, but it looked like thousands.

My heart raced. I knew I had a story to tell, but this was overwhelming. I hadn't been in front of this many people in years.

My mind raced. What would I say? How would I begin my story? I didn't notice the band had been done for a while.

"Mr. Nelson, it's time for you to go. They're waiting for you."

The usher shoved me out into the spotlights.

The stage lights were blinding. I made my way to center stage, and I felt like the whole world was staring at me. I felt naked. The kind of feeling when I used to have dreams as a kid where I'd be at school in my underwear, totally exposed. I was starting to sweat bullets.

I made my way up to the podium that was set up for me and began introducing myself. "Hi, I'm Vincent Nelson. I'm a former pastor, and I want to share my story in the hopes that it will encourage you in your life."

A young lady stood up in the front, pointed at me, and yelled, "You're an adulterer. That's all you really are!"

I panicked and stopped talking, not knowing what to say.

Then a man off to the far right of the stage yelled, "Yeah, you're nothing but a hypocrite and a liar! Why should we listen to your story?"

Paralyzed with fear, I wanted desperately to run off the stage, but instead I said, "No, you have it all wrong. I know I did those things, but it was wrong. I was selfish. I was prideful. I wanted to protect myself from being hurt by others. And I realized I became the god of my own life by doing so." I broke down sobbing. "I was wrong. I was wrong. I was wrong."

"Vince, Vince, wake up. It's okay. You're okay."

I opened my eyes to see the Son looking at me with his hands on my shoulders.

"You're okay. You're here," he said, as if knowing what I was dreaming.

It took a few minutes to snap out of it. He had breakfast ready by the campfire.

I began drinking the coffee he poured, but I wasn't hungry. "I know what we talked about yesterday, about being a representative of the King and bringing his goodness to the world around me. But I just can't do it. I don't want to be a pastor again. I understand I should share the King's goodness with others.

"I want them to experience his goodness and freedom the way I have, but I don't want to be a pastor again and lead others. I screwed that up before. What's to say I wouldn't mess that up again?"

The Son put his coffee cup down. "Vince, let me tell you a secret. You can't blow this. You're a son of the King. Just be his son."

It was hard to look into the Son's eyes as he said that. I couldn't help but avert my eyes and look down at the ground. I knew every word he spoke was true. I knew every word was spoken in love. I even knew I was no longer the selfish person I once was. I was a son of the King. And yet...yet there were moments when I still felt the sharp edge of shame and guilt for the affair, for the DWI, and for hurting so many.

The Son started packing up the campsite.

"Where are we going?" I asked. "Are we going to another campsite tonight?"

The Son looked up from the broken-down tent he was packing and smiled. "Today, Vince, you walk with the King. He asked specifically for you."

My heart felt like it stopped. It was one thing to walk with the Son of the King, but *the King* wanted to walk with me? I wouldn't know what to say. Last time I was in front of him, I felt awkward, naked, like he could see all of me. It was the kind of vulnerability where I wasn't wearing anything, and the top layer of my skin had been peeled off, leaving me totally exposed and overly sensitive.

I think the Son saw the intense look on my face, because he put the tent bag down, walked over to me, and lifted my face to meet his gaze. He then took my arms and held each shoulder tightly. "Vince, this is your destiny. This is your life. This is life...walking with the King. Don't you want to walk with him?

Because the King wants to walk with you."

This time, I received. I received every word the Son spoke. It was no longer about me making my own way. That was a lonely life. A life that was barren and filled with pain. I no longer had to live as a prisoner in shame. I no longer had to live alone. I no longer had anything to hide. And I was loved and embraced just the same. I looked into the Son's eyes and nodded yes.

"Well, great then," he said. "Because look behind you."

I turned around to look, and it wasn't just a king. It wasn't a god like the one I had tried to be in my own life. This was the King of all that was, is, and ever will be. The one who made everything, from stars to planets, from mountain ranges to sunsets. The very one who gave life to all things.

"My Lord, my King." I fell to his feet, realizing the greatness I'd missed all these years.

The King immediately stooped down and put his arms around me. "Vincent, my dearly loved son," he said, lifting me to my feet. "Shall we go for a walk?"

Unable to speak, I nodded yes again and smiled. "Then this way," he said.

He lead the way, through tall pine and oak trees and over brooks, then stopped at a breathtaking vista where I saw white-capped mountains painted with gray, dark blue, and burgundy hues.

Each time I would try to fall behind him, he'd put his arm around me, like the Son would do, and he would lead me, walking by my side, the way a friend and father would his son.

As if knowing everything I had just talked to the Son about, the King stopped and said, "Vince, look at the beauty all around. Look up at the tall majestic mountain behind us. Look over the green valley below. See the pale white moon you can make out in the deep blue sky? Now look deeply into my eyes. Take a deep breath and slowly let it out. You don't have to do anything.

"It's not about you being a pastor. It's not about you trying to be good enough for anyone's approval or trying to avoid being a failure. Just like you've been talking about with my Son the last few days. All you have to do is just be the magnificent son of mine you already are. It's not about what you'll do or don't do right. Vince, you can't blow this."

That was the second time I had heard that.

The King continued, "It's not about your own effort; it's about my effort, my resources, my leadership. It's about just being...belonging. Be my son, the person you already are. You'll lead others to experience my goodness just by walking with me every day. All you need is with me and in me. I'm with you, and you'll hear me lead you and teach you every day, from a place of peace and freedom."

We climbed onto a large boulder overlooking the valley below, and he continued.

"Who you are is not who you were. Who you will be is who you are now. I made you as my noble son. You may not see it now, but if you look through my eyes, you'll see the noble prince you're growing into.

"You're growing up. You're looking more like me every day that you walk with me. Your true nature is being revealed. A person who has huge love, who walks in truthfulness with himself and with others. A child of massive courage! A fearless child whose decisions and actions are courageous, even when you don't know the outcome.

"You know who you are because you know who I am. I am King. So see yourself as you really are, my magnificent glorious son and prince. When I see you, I see me. I see my nature within you. You, Vince, look just like my firstborn Son.

"You have a wonderful future ahead. You are changing the world of darkness you live in because your heart has changed from being dark and selfish to being open and pliable, allowing my voice to breathe life and light into it. You are walking with me now, and where you walk, the goodness of my kingdom is felt. When you receive me and my words, you impact your children's lives, helping them grow into the magnificent people I've made them to be. Do you see that?"

"I remember the time when my children were young," I said. "Nick, my youngest, was afraid of heights, and I was asking him to walk with me on a mountain ridge. He wouldn't do it. But when I lead the way, taking his hand, reassuring him I had him, he began to step out and walk with me, even though the high elevation scared him. My courage gave him courage."

"And do you remember a more recent time, a time that was harder for you, where your courage gave your son courage?" the King asked.

I had to think about it, then I remembered. "I do. It's a little painful of a memory. After my divorce, I felt like such a failure, that I should never remarry because I didn't feel worthy of it. And I could see that the thought of me even dating after the divorce was painful for my kids.

"But then I met Bethany. We were honest about both our failures in life and transparent with who we were. We lived in complete truth with each other and grew to love one another deeply.

"There came the point when I knew I wanted to propose to her. I had worked past the shame of the affairs and my selfish living and saw that I could experience your goodness in my life with Bethany. But I saw it was really hard for Nick.

"And yet I felt that if I wasn't courageous and didn't embrace the goodness you had for me, that he would be stuck in life, living in fear of failed relationships. He would learn a bad lesson, that if you mess up like me, that the King's love, grace, forgiveness, and acceptance as a son of the King couldn't be experienced.

"It took some courage to propose to Bethany because my son could have rejected me as his father for choosing to marry. I needed to model forgiveness for him, yet I knew it could come at the cost of our relationship."

"So what happened?" the King asked.

"My relationship with my son is better than it's ever been. We don't argue. I see him growing closer to you. I see his ability to see through your eyes is amazing. I never knew he was a pioneer like me, but I see it now in our discussions. And he even teaches me things about you now."

The King laughed with a deep roar and gave me a friendly pat on the back. "You're courageous, Vince!

When you walk with me, good things naturally happen. Think about Bethany, your fiancée. You react to her in loving ways because you hear my words guiding your actions. And even when you hurt her feelings, you're quick to understand why and work to have deeper intimacy with her. Even looking back at your past, what do you feel when you think of your parents, going back to your childhood?"

"For my dad, I see a man who taught and modeled how to love deeply and passionately," I said.

"Do you see how that's made it easier for you to receive my love?" the King asked.

"You're right. I do. And I'm incredibly grateful for that."

"And your mom, what about her? How do you feel looking back?"

"Gratitude. I feel appreciation for her. I can see she did the best she could at raising me with the wounds that she carried within her own soul. I see a powerful woman who dealt with those issues and was able to find peace in life, even remarrying a man who would become an encouragement to her. I'm grateful for how she helps other women work through their own fears and move forward in life. And I'm incredibly grateful for the love she shows me. She is a remarkable woman."

"When you walk with me, it's impossible for your heart to stay the same," the King said. "Your heart becomes like my heart. You see people the way I do. You love people the way I do."

"You're right," I said. "I've learned so much with Simon too. You've taught me never say never when it comes to you. I remember when the doctor said Simon would never talk. As a father, I never thought I'd hear the words *I love you, Dad*. But now I hear them every day. I see him playing baseball and basketball with others. He's incredibly loving and kind. You've taught me so much through him. One of the most valuable lessons is don't confine a person to the dreams you have for them; let the dreams and purpose you've placed within them grow. It will always be beautiful."

"I've seen you heal even with your ex-wife," the King said. "I was so proud of you when you had a joint birthday party for Simon turning eighteen. You've let go of any resentment you've felt towards her and partnered with her as parents to raise your boys in the most loving environment possible."

"When you listen and respond to me, the people around you see me because they see you," he said. "People hear my hope because they hear you. People feel me wipe their tears because you wipe their tears. People hear and experience my freedom because they experience it through you. You are my heart and my hands to them."

"But I have to be honest," I said. "When I do hurt Bethany's feelings or act selfishly, in any way, it sends me right back to the shame, guilt, and failure of my past. I just want to beat myself up when I do that. Don't you see that?" I asked. "It sometimes still brings up the feelings of shame from the affair, from the lying, the DWI, and all the damage I caused. If I'm even more honest, there are times I don't feel I'm even worthy to be your son."

"Vincent, if you think that your failures in the past disqualify you from my love and being a part of my family, then you are extremely arrogant. It's prideful to think you have any ability to be good enough to become an heir of mine. It's not about you; it's about my Son, the Son, who gave his life for you. It's about embracing him and allowing him to embrace all of you.

"You can't make yourself a son. You're a son simply because you receive my firstborn Son. Vince, you didn't make yourself into my son, no more than a servant can ever do enough good things to become a son of a King. I made you. You're my son because of me."

Rivers of truth and life poured into my soul as he spoke. Wave after wave of words penetrated every facet of my being. I breathed it all in. I received all he was saying, and for the first time in my life, I was walking with the King and listening with all of my soul.

As I reflected, I still wondered...

"My King—" I caught myself trying to speak in the way he spoke to me. "Dad, how can I avoid the pitfalls of the past as I live in the present?"

I think he enjoyed me calling him Dad because he got the biggest smile when I did. And I realized the word Dad was growing easier to say; it was the truth after all.

"Avoid the pitfalls of the past?" he said, repeating my question. "It's simple... Follow me, Vincent. Walk with me daily. It's about intimacy with me, not what you do, but who I am and whose you are. There's nothing I desire more than having an intimate, daily relationship with you.

"Intimacy is simply about being fully known and knowing the other person completely. It's about living in complete truth and love with each other, not hiding thoughts, feelings, or actions.

"It's about inviting the other person to know everything there is to know about you, the great, the bad, the things that make you happy or sad, and your dreams, your desires. It's being fully laid bare and still being embraced, imperfections and all. That's what love is. Vincent, the truth is, I know all there is to know about you. But I want you to want to be known and not want to hide anything. I embrace all of you, just as you are.

"Intimacy is just like a coin, with two sides. There's the one side of you that you are already aware of. The other side of it is... I want to be known by you, Vincent. Entirely. When I say I want to walk with you daily, I want you to know my thoughts, how I feel about things. I want you to know my heart for you and have access to all I own simply because I love you."

Wow, that was a lot to take in. He was speaking the thing my heart had always longed for but was too scared to ask. And yet, here he was, wanting the same thing and asking that of me, to walk in intimacy with me.

I looked off into the valley and the world below. "But Dad," I said, "just like that whole bad nightmare wearing only underwear at school in my childhood dream, it's hard being vulnerable like that."

The King laughed. "Well, the kind of vulnerability I'm talking about isn't really like you being naked at school in your dream, but maybe it's close. It's uncomfortable. But it's love, my love, that will remove your fear of vulnerability, helping you experience that it's safe to be known. Being known is allowing me to embrace all of you.

"You've come to a place of brokenness and surrender, where you feel like you've lost control of your life and you're exposed for the world to see. You feel unsafe. You believe brokenness is a weakness, something you need to hide or run from. But brokenness isn't the same thing as being worthless.

"Brokenness doesn't mean you're disposable. Brokenness is what holds you close to my heart like a baby carrier holds a child close to its parent's chest. Brokenness leads to dependence on me, and connects you to me relationally, your true source of life. Learning how to live truthfully with yourself allows you to see your vulnerability and weakness, and causes you to see your need for me.

"It's the reminder that life flows from me, not knowledge of me, or principles, or your own strength. It's your attachment to me, intimacy walked out daily with me, moment by moment, and that makes the brokenness in you beautiful. It changes it from a weakness and turns it into life and strength for you.

"You were broken by others when you were sexually abused as a child. You were broken in your own attempt to protect yourself and manipulate people to provide what you thought you needed. All of that caused great shame. But Vince"—he gently lifted my head up until my gaze met his—"I don't see a shameful person. I don't see an ugly heart. I see nobility, beauty, and purpose in you.

"I see my dearly loved Son. As you embrace your dependence on me, you'll see yourself through my eyes, and you'll help others experience the same with me.

"As you've learned, Vince, I am Life itself. All you need is always found in me. See your weakness and brokenness as a reminder of whose you are, a child connected to his Daddy and King, with me right by your side, with all you need. And I'll lead you and guide you. When you live with me, you will always have life, for I am Life."

By the edge of the cliff, we found a huge strong tree with a nice slope at its base to lean against. We both sat back and relaxed. Then I shut my eyes, reflecting on all he had shared and letting it sink in.

Intimacy, yes, I understood it now, was the foundation my life had been missing. I hid my shame from the King for decades, trying to hide from him and others out of fear of rejection.

But no more.

I was sitting next to the King. He knew all of me. And I wanted to know more of him. As I drifted off to sleep, peace flooded my soul. I felt more rested than I had my entire life.

Truth is a harder mountain to climb than illusion.
At the top are the winds of freedom. Persevere!

—BETHANY WILLIAMS AND VINCENT NELSON

Chapter 11

TRUTH AND LOVE, THE PATHWAY TO INTIMACY

"Sex!" the King shouted.

His voice shook me awake.

"What?" I sat there rubbing my eyes. *Is he really going to talk about sex? Well, this could be interesting.* "How long have I been asleep?"

"About an hour," he said. "I figured you needed to rest for a bit after all we shared."

"So…why did you wake me up with the word *sex*?" I asked.

"To get your attention, of course! It seems to have worked." He chuckled. "Let me help you understand what true intimacy is, because the world around you has often gotten it wrong, thinking of intimacy as sex. Yes, that's one form of intimacy, but it's just a very small part.

"Intimacy is about being fully known and knowing the other completely. It's about experiencing all there is to experience with that other person, daily, in an ongoing relationship.

And how you live in that kind of relationship is simple: it's living in truth and love.

"You've heard it said that you should be truthful. But did you know that truth is much more than just a concept?"

I had to think about it for a while, then I said I remembered reading before that the Son said, "I am the way, the truth, and the life" (John 14:6 NLT).

"That's right. Truth isn't just a concept or a principle to be applied to your life. If it was, it could be easily discarded like so many try to do. If I was just a concept, then moral relativism might apply. Meaning truth is what you think truth is, from your point of view.

"But truth isn't a concept.

"I Am Truth. My very nature as King is that all life and knowledge flows from me. I created the stars and the galaxies. I created the largest universe down to the smallest atom and quark. I even created smaller things than quarks and bigger things than galaxies that scientists have yet to discover.

"I created thought and words and established absolutes. All of those things were created out of my nature and my being, simply by breathing them into existence. And the same is true with all of humanity. As one ancient philosopher said, 'In him we live and move and have our being.'

"I Am Truth. So when you walk with me, you are living in truth. It's in truth that you experience life and freedom, the fullness of life."

The King stopped walking for a moment, knelt down, and drew a line in the dirt with a stick. At the right side of the line, he wrote the word *Truth*.

Truth

"Vincent, do you know what happens when you chose to reject Truth?" He wrote the word *Illusion* on the left-hand side:

_ILLusion_____Truth_____

The King started walking down the mountain again, and I followed close. I could tell he wanted me to think about those words, *Truth* and *Illusion*.

As we continued walking, I was getting thirsty. I could hear what sounded like the roar of a river ahead, but it still sounded far off. Fortunately, I notice a small pond close by. I left the path following the King and was bending down to drink out of it when his voice boomed at me.

"Vincent, stop! Don't drink that," he yelled. "It will make you sick! There's some clean water up ahead."

"But this looks clear to me," I yelled back.

Walking up to me, he said, "It may look clear, but clear and clean are two different things. Look around you, pay attention."

I noticed a dead bird by the side of the small pond, then spotted a few small dead animals.

"The water is clear," he said, "but it will actually make you sick, even kill you if you drink enough of it. Notice the pond doesn't have an inlet or an outlet to it. The water in it is stagnant and has enough bad bacteria in it to quickly kill off small animals. Just because it looks good, doesn't mean it is good. Take a look through that clearing, though."

Through a gap in some trees, I saw a waterfall and river glistening in the sun, about a quarter of a mile away. We made our way toward it, and my Dad told me it was good to drink.

"Now, this is good water. It's healthy because it's continually flowing and being purified. Truth and illusion are similar to the pond and the river. Truth, like the river, has continual life to it.

"When you're living in it, it lives in you. It nourishes your mind, your heart, and your soul. It guides your emotions and decisions. It causes you to change. Just like plants that receive good water grow and change into the beautiful thing they were intended to be.

"Truth addresses your misconceptions of life and corrects it. Just like you've been learning about your worth with me. In the past, you saw yourself as a failure and disposable. Now you are seeing yourself as noble and wanting to help others. You're willing to grow, and you listen to the truth when you're wrong, and you ask for help to change.

"When you encounter truth, it changes you. You will never be the same as you were. When you encounter me, you'll never be the same.

"Truth helps you become more of the magnificent and noble child of mine that you already were. It removes the obstacles of illusionary less than living and helps you live in your true identity and nobility.

"Illusionary living, on the other hand, leads to the same thing as the pond did. Over time, it hurts and it kills. It keeps you from experiencing the beauty of your purpose. When you choose to abandon truth, you choose to live in something that's void of intimacy with others, of life and of your purpose.

"Illusionary living is like eating the breadcrumbs of life off the floor when instead you could be dining on the prime rib of Truth at the King's table. In dating relationships and marriage, it happens when people chose to hide who they really are from the other and pretend to be someone they are not. Why do you think so many people towards the end of failed relationships say, 'I guess I never really knew them'?

It's because that person never revealed their self, for whatever fear-based reason.

"Or in jobs, people lying about who they are on a resume, or presenting themselves as having experience in a certain field when they don't? Maybe they're choosing those actions to steal from others and companies what wasn't honestly theirs to begin with.

"Consider how many people destroy their lives by continually drinking the water from the pond until the truth about them is found out, and the company and people lose their trust in them. Then they end up losing their career, hurting their family, and more.

"Illusionary living always leads to death. Sometimes it may be a slow death, decades that lead to death of relationships, careers, and their future. But it always leads to death.

"Living in the truth, walking with me daily, always leads to life, removes obstacles, and leads you into a greater level of freedom than before. No hiding. No lying. No need to look over your shoulder. Peace. Peace with me. Peace with others. Peace with yourself."

Sunlight danced through the swaying trees above, hitting my face. I felt alive. I felt destiny within my soul rising. I could understand all he was saying and knew what he meant about truth changing me for the better.

My relationship with my sons was better than it had ever been. My relationship with my wife, Bethany, was growing in beautiful ways as we experienced the intimacy that my Dad and King was talking about. And I saw people at work in a different light. I could see what fears they were dealing with and could hear the King talk about how to extend his goodness to them in the way they needed it most.

But most of all, I felt deep love between the King and me. I could hear his heart for me and receive all he wanted to share. And he listened to me, to my heart, my struggles, my joy—anything I wanted to share.

The way I lived my past life was full of illusion. I pretended I didn't have fear. I pretended I could have healthy relationships with people. I worked hard to be admired, to be followed. And in truth, I lived in an illusion of life.

What looked like a successful life that people admired was really just like the pond—lifeless and toxic because it wasn't tied to real life. It wasn't tied to the King.

"But Dad, a lot of the time living in truth is downright terrifying," I said. "I mean, if I've been living a lie and want to be truthful, that means I'm exposing myself and will probably face consequences for my actions."

"Probably," the King said. "But the truth is, you'll eventually experience consequences for your actions even if you don't live in honesty. Eventually, it will kill you."

He was right about that. The way I lived my life was a perfect illustration for that.

"Wouldn't you rather live in truth and experience my peace and my embrace, knowing you may have to face a little pain?" he asked.

"Of course," I said. Intimacy with him was now the most important thing. "I chose to live in freedom, no matter what I have to face living in truth."

"Let me ask you a question. Why was it you were willing to face the truth of your selfish living and listen to me?"

I thought about it for a while. "Because I knew I could trust you."

The King smiled and looked back at me. "Vincent, I love you. You are my dearly loved child."

I knew he meant it. I could feel it. I could see it looking back at my life—even when others hurt me, even when I was as hurting myself, he was always there, loving me and trying to guide me when I listened.

He bent down again and started writing in the dirt. This

time he drew the same line with the words *Illusion* and *Truth*. But he added another line, with the word *Love* at the top and *Fear* at the bottom.

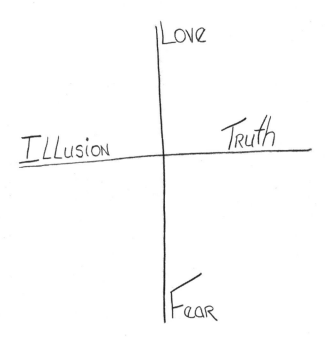

"Vincent, as much as I Am Truth, I am also the fullness of Love. To move from illusion to truth, you have to receive Love. Love is what displaces fear. And love is what creates trust. Trust is the foundation for being vulnerable, where it's safe to be completely laid bare. Love makes it possible for you and others to receive truth.

"You knew I was there for you when you were completely broken. You had experienced love from me in the past, and so you were willing to intently listen to my words of forgiveness from others who were counseling you after your divorce.

"Trust is what opened your heart and ears to not only receive that you had been selfish, but to understand why you

had been selfish. It also moved you towards being courageous enough to ask for forgiveness for hurting others: your
ex-wife, your children, the woman you had the affair with,
church leaders. And my love gave you the strength to leave
behind the shame of your failure and be able to receive the
worth and nobility I had placed within your soul.

"Because of love, you received truth, and truth started to
remove the obstacles in your path and help you live as my
dearly loved and noble son, with a fresh empowerment for
living out your unique purpose of sharing my goodness as
only Vincent can do."

I think I must have kneeled there for minutes. It felt like
hours. Those last words brought it all together. I saw how I
lived my past life and why I lived it that way. I saw my present
nobility and was growing to live in that more, every day.

But more than that, I was with the King! I was with my
Dad, and he was with me. This was Truth. This was Love.
This was true intimacy—nothing hidden, fully free, fully
embraced.

I embraced him like I had never done before. Tears ran
down my cheeks. But this time they weren't tears of shame
or pain. They were tears of joy. The air I was breathing was
freedom, and it was the freshest air I'd ever felt permeate my
lungs.

I could see how small I was in light of humanity in the
course of human history. One single speck of sand in the
largest sandy desert. But I also felt huge. I wasn't Vince the
failed pastor, husband, and father. I was a warrior, a noble, a
champion. I was a child of the King!

Slowly we stood up as he embraced me again.

Wiping the tears from my eyes, he laughed and looked me
square in the eye. "Yep, you're my boy."

We continued walking, his huge hand taking my small
hand in his.

"Vincent, your destiny awaits. And you're not alone. I am with you, always," he said. "I enjoy our intimate walks."

"And we get to do them every day," I said with a smile.

"Moment by moment," said the King, my Dad. "Walk with me. Listen to my heart. I'm listening to yours. I have so many things to share with you. And I'll guide you, always."

As we walked down the path, the Friend who had been with me throughout my life joined us. Seeing him this time, I noticed he looked just like the King and his Son. He had always been faithful to speak the King's truth and love; I just didn't always receive it. But now, it was different. I was listening. I was receiving. And I wanted it.

A few moments later, I noticed Bethany farther down the hiking trail, along with one of the Kilimanjaro guides.

I ran to catch up with them. "I haven't seen you in a couple of days."

"What are you talking about? You've only been behind us a few minutes," Bethany said.

I looked around and didn't see the King, and yet I could still feel him with me, and the Friend who always counseled me. Had it really only been a few minutes? It had felt like a lifetime.

I walked off Mount Kilimanjaro a different man that day. I would never walk a day alone again. I understood now, and I would listen to the voice of the King, letting his Truth and Love guide me.

I felt destiny in each footstep.

Each footstep was an opportunity to receive the King and to share his goodness. Each relationship a chance to live in the truth of who I am and to embrace others with the King's embrace. I would never live life the same way again. I would never be the same old Vincent I was. After all, I was a...*child of the King.*

See the summit, not the challenge; see the next step, not the next mile. Live life as an adventure and you'll experience a lifetime of summits.

—Vincent Nelson

Epilogue

A LETTER TO THE READER

What do you have to let go of?

When Bethany asked me to hike the Kalalau Trail in Kawai with her in November of 2015, I was all in, even knowing it was listed as one of the most beautiful and most dangerous hikes in the United States. It's the place where Steven Spielberg filmed some extraordinary footage for the movie *Jurassic Park*.

What I failed to hear her say was that it's also considered one of the hardest hikes in the US. With over nineteen ascents and descents on the trail, it kicked my behind for sure, not to mention I was out of shape. Our trip quickly got very real as I was in terrible pain, throwing up and moving very slow.

I would later find out I had a bad allergy to gluten, which was present in all I ate. It made my joints ache, my gut wrench, and my head pound with migraines. All of this on the trail, including the worst stinky feet you've ever smelled, and she still accepted me, still loved me, even if she did make me wash my feet in ice cold water.

Prior to our hike, with Bethany's encouragement and help, I had begun prepping for the book back in March of 2015, but it was after our hike on the Kalalau trail that I began writing the first chapters of this book.

Over the next year and a half, I lived life to the fullest with Bethany, from experiencing great joy as we summited Mount Kilimanjaro, the tallest freestanding mountain in the world, to proposing to her at the top of the mountain, to the beautiful wedding we experienced in September of 2016.

Through the journey Bethany and I took, I would write in different locations, experiencing similar joy and pain as I would write each page, reflecting on failures and the ultimate eternal embrace that was mine from the King.

This whole journey has been about brokenness that leads to surrender, finally allowing my heart to let go of the fear of rejection and pain, and finally receive love. And as I receive, I'm finally able to receive the truth of who I am and receive the embrace of my Dad, my Creator God.

Now the journey continues for me as I enjoy a daily journey with Him as his son, listening to him, walking with him, and experiencing the magnificent destiny he has for me in my life with Bethany, my boys, my stepchildren, our friends, and those I work with—wherever my King leads.

Part of that journey has sometimes been painful. I love how freedom feels, and I know that freedom is found in being truthful. It's been hard revisiting the past, asking for forgiveness of those I've hurt. I asked for forgiveness for the pain I caused my ex-wife. I asked for forgiveness from my boys, who are my joy and passion. And I asked for forgiveness for the lies and illusion of promising love to the woman I had an affair with.

I know I'll still have painful days along the journey as I face my selfishness and seek to give honor and love where I've hurt people who are made in the King's image. The reason I can face that and not run and hide is simply love. The love of the King is received in my heart. Even when I fail, I'm still loved, and that empowers my heart to respond no matter what I face.

The love and truth journey, what Bethany and I have come to call The Intimacy Journey, has become the foundation for this book. It's the foundation of our lives. Bethany and I began getting to know each other several years ago after being introduced by our mutual friend, Tammy Kling.

Bethany is beautiful but not the type I would normally have chosen for myself. She was a corporate executive who had written six books and looked very successful and glamorous from the outside looking in.

I was intimidated and thought she was probably materialistic. She had similar reservations about me too! I was a former pastor after all. She was wondering if I'd be judgmental and religious, condemning her if she didn't live a certain way.

From the beginning we chose to be brutally honest, sharing all of our failures in our marriages, our selfish actions, the idiosyncrasies of our personalities, and more. We tried to run each other off, but something strange happened. The opposite occurred.

We didn't run away. We drew closer to each other as we lived in complete truth with each other. We found it was safe to open up. We both had failed in life, so why would we judge each other for our pasts? In fact, we found that we accepted and understood each other—broken, marred souls and all.

In that, love began to grow. We found as we were kind and encouraging, we would share more. We found that we could challenge each other and be truthful and not run and hide. It was a journey of living truthfully with each other. Finding love encouraged us to grow and be even more transparent. We found intimacy.

As we were dating and learning more, we began shooting videos, sharing all about our failures and our learnings together on social media. And yes, we were totally transparent, even talking about things like my affair. We called it The Intimacy Journey.

It was on that journey where I learned truth is more than a concept. Truth is God himself. Jesus said, "I am…the truth" in John 14:6. The Bible says, "God is love" in 1 John 4:8. Truth and love are the keys to experiencing intimacy.

As we were truthful with ourselves and God, our relationship with each other grew.

I began reflecting over the years of being a pastor and seeing that so much of it was just knowledge for me. It wasn't about intimacy with God because it was about life on my own terms. I missed things like Psalm 139, which paints a magnificent picture of God's intimate hand in our lives. I missed Proverbs 3:5–6, that wasn't about having head knowledge about God, but rather about having heart knowledge. Verse 6 says, "Seek his will in all you do, and he will show you which path to take" (NLT).

As God was rebuilding my life, giving me courage to accept my noble identity of being made "in his own image" (Genesis 1:27 NLT), it took me back to the Garden of Eden, where Adam and Eve were completely naked and completely known physically, emotionally, and spiritually. They were known and embraced by each other; they were known and knew and embraced God their Creator.

In this place, they experienced deep intimacy. It was a place of security and safety where they could live and grow as children of the King of the Universe and live out their purpose and destiny.

If you've read Genesis, then you know there were also two trees. One was the Tree of Life. The other was the Tree of Knowledge; more accurately called the Tree of Knowledge of Good and Evil. It wasn't until Adam and Eve ate of the Tree of Knowledge that intimacy was destroyed.

Adam and Eve hid from each other. They felt shame in their nakedness and covered themselves. In essence, they hid from each other, afraid of being rejected. They also hid from God, their Creator. They no longer were connected to the Tree of Life, to God himself, but they were connected to the Tree of Knowledge by trying to be their own god.

It became about "doing" rather than "being." It was about being "good enough" to be accepted, about doing enough good things to measure up. It was also about avoiding doing evil things like hurting others. In so doing, they lost sight of being children of the King, from whom flows their very life and identity.

I had missed this. It was about my knowledge. It was about how to meet my needs my way. Serving others in the church was about proving my value to myself, to my King, and to others. It was about how to make myself happy and give my life value. I failed at it all.

The darkness of my own heart would often pop up like that proverbial beach ball, smacking me in the face. But once I allowed love and truth in, I finally began to experience real freedom. I finally saw it was impossible to ever make my life into something that felt fulfilled, good, and worthy. It wasn't until I lost everything—my family, my ministry, my job, my integrity, the trust others had in me—that I was finally able to stop trying to do anything other than receive God's love and enjoy being the magnificent, noble son he'd already made me into.

For me, living in intimacy with the King is the foundation for life. Bethany and I have found that the foundation of intimacy, Love and Truth, are essential to experiencing healthy relationships of all kinds.

Soon we will write a book about real intimacy—what it looks like in relationships, where we guide people to experience deeper intimacy with others.

As this book comes to a close, though, my heart and my passion for you is simply this...that you'll experience what it means to be a child of the King!

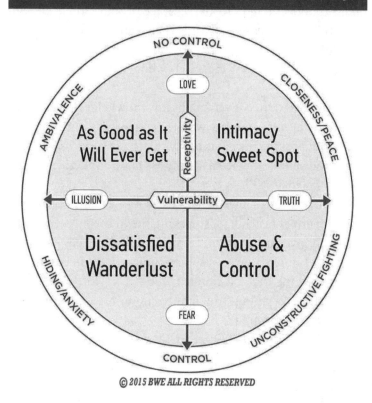

Does this book leave unanswered questions for you?

I hope so. If life were about the destination, then it would be about knowledge. But it's not. It's about the journey, an intimate journey between you and your Dad, who happens to be the King.

Ask him your questions. He's listening. Are you listening to his heart? He wants to share.

You are loved, my dear friend. You matter, and you are magnificent! It doesn't matter where you've been or what you've done. You're not forgotten. You are priceless. You are precious. You are unique. You have a destiny that this world needs to experience.

Open your heart to receive his embrace. Walk with him and experience what it means to be a child of the King.

Child
—of—
The King

ABOUT VINCENT NELSON

Vincent Nelson was a pastor and leader for over 17 years. He spent more than 20 years in inspirational speaking, and developing people towards their purpose. His impactful speeches and motivational messages catapulted him into leadership positions by the age of 30. He traveled the world planting micro-enterprises that funded orphanages and churches for humanitarian purposes.

He found his life's calling after a total life melt down that resulted in the loss of his marriage, his job, and his freedom. His calling and purpose is to free individuals to find the incredible nobility and destiny that each person has. He believes that you can reach your full purpose and be a powerful catalyst for changing the world.

Vincent is remarried and lives in Dallas with his wife and children. He has two boys, privileged to have a special needs child to rediscover the world through his eyes.

Freedom Speeches

With over 20 years of inspiration speaking, Vincent is passionate about helping people find freedom from deep soul issues which keep them from living as the incredible miracle they already are. His motivational, heartfelt and practical messages include topics like overcoming childhood sexual abuse, failed marriages, deep shame, relationship loss, job loss, suicidal thoughts, control issues, loss of purpose and the discovery of what it means to be a child of the King.

Freedom Coaching

Vincent provides Freedom Coaching for those seeking one on one coaching for overcoming past issues that have held you back from living in freedom and moving into your life's purpose and legacy.

To discuss how Vincent can be an encouragement to you and your organization, visit
Website: www.vincentnelsonauthor.com
Email: vincentnelson@me.com
Facebook: Vince Nelson
Twitter: Livingsonship
Blog: www.livingsonship.com
YouTube: Vincent Nelson
Instagram: Vince_soul_healer

FREEDOM RETREATS & FREEDOM COACHING FOR RELATIONSHIPS

Her Story...

Bethany Williams has over 30 years as a corporate growth agent and executive coach to C-suite executives and entrepreneurs across the globe. Known for her TedX talk, Bethany has written 7 books. Her resume includes senior leadership and acting as a growth agent for companies like IDX, GE, Perot Systems, PWC and ZirMed. Known as the 'CEO Whisperer,' top leaders seek her out to listen to their ideas and advise them on growth strategies. She has a long track record of doubling company revenues and finding weaknesses that prevent company growth. Coupled with her powerful corporate background and wisdom gained from the loss of two husbands, being a single mom, and overcoming physical pain and limitations, Bethany's strength in relational coaching is helping people identify their areas for growth and the steps necessary to experience deep meaningful relationships.

His Story...

Vincent Nelson was a pastor for 17 years, helping thousands of people identify the soul issues within (issues of emotions, the mind, and the will) that keep them from experiencing healthy relationships. As Vincent has walked through his own recovery from deep painful childhood issues of mistrust and isolation and the selfish actions that resulted from them, he's learned the steps necessary to becoming a healthy individual. It's those steps that lead a person from striving to rest with the discovery of the innate value that already resides within, creating the healthy foundation for vibrant relationships.

Together...

Several years ago Vincent and Bethany met and began something they call the truth and love journey. They began a video series on YouTube and then on their website called The Intimacy Journey...a place where you can be known fully, know another fully, and still be completely embraced. They began sharing their own stories of relationship failure and the steps needed to experience real intimacy.

Together Vincent and Bethany make a powerful coaching team, identifying the issues that hold people back from meaningful relationships and provide the steps to experience deep, lasting intimacy. To learn more about the unique Freedom Retreats and Coaching they provide, in addition to their video series and other relationship material, go to:

www.bethanyawilliams.com/the-intimacy-journey
Email: vincentnelson@me.com

The Intimacy Journey Video Series - Season 1
YouTube: The Intimacy Journey – Journey to Eden

The Intimacy Journey Video Series - Season 2 and Beyond
www.bethanyawilliams.com/the-intimacy-journey

See Vincent's travel guidebook
The Kalalau Trail Guidebook
Information to make your upcoming hike in Kauai amazing

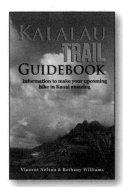

Avid adventurers Bethany Williams and Vince Nelson take you on a tour of the Kalalau Trail in the Kauai Hawaii. Known as one of the 10 most beautiful, hardest and dangerous hikes in the US, they traverse this difficult trail and give you advice and inspiration for your journey.

Though they have spent more time in the boardroom than in nature, both have traveled the globe in their pursuit to find joy and inspiration in the great outdoors.

Bethany is host of *Home Made Money* and *3 Days to a Raise* TV shows and Vince is the producer of the shows.

Discover a part of the island that you never knew existed, and journey to the real garden of Eden.

Available on www.Amazon.com.